STEVENAGE PAST

Stevenage V.E. Day 50th anniversary parade, Monday 8 May 1995. The procession, which included the greatest number of Dunkirk veterans in any parade outside London, marched from Ditchmore Lane (formerly London Road) through the High Street to the War Memorial on the Bowling Green. It then proceeded to the Bury Mead, where a commemorative service was held.

STEVENAGE PAST

Margaret Ashby

Phillimore

1995

Published by
PHILLIMORE & CO. LTD.,
Shopwyke Manor Barn, Chichester, West Sussex

ISBN 0 85033 970 7

Printed and bound in Great Britain by
BIDDLES LTD.
Guildford, Surrey

Contents

List of Illustrations

Frontispiece: V.E. Day 50th anniversary parade, Monday 8 May 1995

vii

Acknowledgements

I am extremely grateful to the many people who have helped in the preparation of this book. It would not have been possible without them.

The following have kindly allowed me to reproduce photographs: Joan Amis, 13, 15, 32, 45, 55, 62, 68, 78, 81, 84, 92, 94-6, 112; Jean Archer, 64; the late Denis Boorman, 124; the family of Lt. Col. J.D. Chalmers, 120; Peg Charlton, 88, 89; J. Elliott, 104; Roy Findley, frontispiece; Jack Franklin, 57; Mim French, 56; Hertfordshire Record Office, 24; Huntingdon Record Office, 41; Philip Ireton, 119; Ian Lines, 80; Brian Norman, 16; James Poston, 21, 115, 117; John Richardson, 8, 10, 18, 22, 44, 52, 54, 61, 65, 66, 76, 79, 83; Merle Saunders, 71-5, 77; Mrs. P. Shepherd, 108, 109; Richard Stephens, Secretary of the Old Alleynians' Association, 50, 51, 114; Stevenage Museum, 1, 12, 20, 23, 48, 49, 57, 60, 63, 67, 82, 86, 110, 111, 113, 121 and Mrs. L. Wheatley, 25, 29, 31, 33, 37, 38, 69, 70, 90, 99, 101, 105-7.

Every effort has been made to trace copyright owners and obtain their permission to reproduce illustrations. If there are any errors or omissions I apologise to those concerned and ask their forbearance. The jacket illustration was painted by Ken Woodruff, to whom I extend grateful thanks. I also would like to record my appreciation of the help given by the following, in supplying information or in other ways; E.J. Bowers, Virginia Cole, Roy Findley, J. Franklin, Betty Game, Joan Hale, John Hepworth, Andrew Newton, Arthur Richards, Iain Sillars, Mary Spicer, Christine Starr.

A special word of thanks must go to Joan Williams, who might reasonably have given up trying to teach me history many years ago.

Any errors are entirely my own work.

Chapter 1

Chronology

c.A.D. 43 - *c*.A.D. 400

During the Roman occupation of Britain, there was a settlement in the district now known as Stevenage. Roman pottery has been found in Whomerley Wood, near Sish Lane and in Walkern Road.

c.100

A wealthy Roman family, possibly farming locally, built a row of burial mounds beside the road which was later to become the Great North Road. These burial mounds, or 'Six Hills' as they are usually known, have for centuries been landmarks to travellers entering Stevenage from the south. The Great North Road probably began life as a prehistoric track, but it was certainly straightened, drained and properly surfaced by the Romans,

an improvement which was to shape the whole future of the town.

c.193 - 263

Exciting new evidence of a Roman presence came to light in 1986, during the building of Chells Manor Village. 2,579 coins covering the period A.D. 193 to 263 were discovered buried in an earthenware pot in the fields between Chells and Walkern. Some coins show the head of the little-known Emperor Pacatian, whose brief, uneasy reign lasted for a few months in A.D. 249. Although most histories of the Roman Empire ignore him, he will not easily be forgotten in Stevenage, where Pacatian Way road, and the nearby public house, *The Emperor's Head*, are named after him.

1 A Roman coin hoard unearthed in a field during the building of Chells Manor Village in 1986.

c.383 - c.800

Saxon settlers arrived in north Hertfordshire. At some time during this period a village of wooden, thatched huts was built on the hill-top overlooking the Roman Great North Road. A church, also built of wood and a Bury, or manor house, were added in due course and their successors, St Nicholas' Church and the Old Bury, occupy the same site today. The Saxons gave their village the name *Stigenace*, or *Stithenac*, which is generally accepted as meaning 'at the strong oak.' In the early days of the village, the thickly wooded slopes of their hill protected them from attack, at a time when it was too dangerous to live in exposed situations.

Other Saxon villages and farmsteads grew up in the surrounding woodland, including those at Chells, Woolenwick, Homele (now spelled Whomerley) and Broadwater. The village of Shephall also has Saxon origins.

c.800 - c.1066

Danish invasions brought much bitter fighting to Hertfordshire. Stevenage was very close to the boundary of Danelaw, the line established in the reign of Alfred the Great which separated Danish rule to the east from English rule to the west. The number of places in east Hertfordshire named Dane End is an indication of this line. The nearest Dane End to Stevenage is a mere two miles away from St Nicholas' Church, between Weston and Walkern. This makes it extremely unlikely that the villagers of Stigenace could have avoided involvement in the continual battles and skirmishes. Yet the only surviving link with those gory days appears to be the name Gunnell's Wood, originating from the Danish Gonnildesgrave, which means 'the wood belonging to a woman called Gunnhild'. Over the centuries local people have speculated about other possible evidence of a Danish

2 St Nicholas' Church, Old Bury and cottages, *c.*1980. The field in the foreground has been built over since this photograph was taken.

3 St Nicholas' Church and Old Bury, *c*.1985.

4 The Old Bury beside St Nicholas' Church.

presence in the district, and the naming of parts of the New Town centre, such as Danestrete, Daneshill House and the former *Longship* public house in St George's Way followed this tradition.

c.1062

King Edward the Confessor gave Stevenage to the Abbey of St Peter at Westminster. It is likely that from this date St Nicholas' Church no longer had to rely on travelling priests, but was served by priests from Westminster, who may also have set up a monastic foundation in Stevenage, beside what is now Rectory Lane.

1086

The survey of land and property in England, ordered by William the Conqueror and recorded for all time in Domesday Book, shows that the Abbot of Westminster was confirmed as the lord of the manor of Stevenage. The population of the village was probably at least one hundred people, who made their living directly from the land. They kept cattle on meadowland they had cleared from the forest and pigs which fed on beechmast and acorns under the trees. The villagers had seven ploughs between them and possibly about 1,600 acres of arable land on which they grew wheat, oats, barley and peas.

At the time of the Domesday Survey, the Abbot of St Albans held Shephall. Chells was divided among the rich and powerful Norman landowners, Robert of Bayeux, Peter de Valognes, Robert Gernon and Geoffrey de Bech, but one small part of it was still occupied by the Saxon Aluric Busch, who paid a halfpenny yearly for the privilege. Peter de Valognes and Robert Gernon also each owned land in Woolenwick.

c.1100 - c.1130

The tower of St Nicholas' Church was built of flint and stone, to serve not only for religious purposes, but also as a stronghold where the villagers could shelter from attack.

5 St Nicholas' Church, showing the door in the tower which opens into a space above the present roof, indicating that at some time in the past the nave roof was higher.

6 The Bowling Green at the fork of the Great North Road and Hitchin Road. The man walking along Hitchin Road with a briefcase is probably on his way to the railway station in Julian's Road, *c.*1900.

1213

Nicholas FitzSimon was appointed the first recorded Rector of Stevenage by the Abbot of Westminster.

*c.*1200 - 1281

The population of Stevenage moved from its original hilltop site to settle beside the Roman road, around what is now the Bowling Green.

1275

Ivo de Homle held land in Stevenage.

5 June 1281

King Edward I granted the Abbot of Westminster, as lord of the manor, the right to hold a weekly market and a yearly fair 'in perpetuity' at Stevenage. Over the years, the booths and stalls of travelling merchants became permanent dwellings in the part of the High Street known as Middle Row. Stevenage market continued to be held in the open space at the north end of Middle Row until the 1950s,

at the place where the town's market cross had previously stood for nearly six centuries.

1310

King Edward II had a prison in Stevenage.

1312

A school existed in Stevenage. The Westminster Abbey accounts record details of the expenses incurred by William le Rous, a pupil.

1315

A survey of all his land in Stevenage was made on behalf of the Abbot of Westminster. Twelve citizens of the town were sworn in as a jury to give a true account of land and property occupation. They were William de Chelse, Roger Trot, Roger atte Upehende, John Shush (or Sish or Shish), Thomas atte Grave, Robert atte Cherch, Richard Feveral, John Couppere, Eustace atte Dane, Roger le Rene, John atte Hern and Roger atte Grave. Their names often

7 Middle Row originated in medieval times as the booths and stalls of itinerant traders which later became permanent, 1991.

8 Stevenage Fair in 1906.

9 Middle Row and the High Street, traditional site for the crockery stall at Stevenage Fair, 1975.

10 Baker Street in 1933.

indicated whereabouts they lived, or held property: Chells, Trott's Hill, Sishes and the lane leading to it.

Nearly 140 heads of household were listed in the survey, from which it has been calculated that the total population of Stevenage was then approximately one thousand people.

The amount of rent due from each tenant is also included in the report. Peter de Bedewell paid 5s. 4d. for his one messuage and half a virgate of land (a messuage was a house and garden, a virgate about 30 acres); John Shepherd paid 3d. for his messuage, but Henry the Shoemaker paid 2s. for his. Women as well as men held property and land; Parnel, daughter of Robert le Flessmonger, paid 6d. per annum for her messuage and Mabel Duff paid 12s. for hers.

c.1330 - c.1450

St Nicholas' Church was enlarged, to provide wider aisles and a new chancel. Brilliantly coloured scenes from the Bible were painted on the new walls and later new stalls and misericords were added in the chancel. Most striking of all the changes was the building of a spire to surmount the flint tower. Robert Trow Smith describes it as 'one of the most graceful in the county, built upon a structure which is a miracle of timber framing almost worthy of comparison with the intricacies of the chapter house roof at York.'

1349

The Black Death reached Stevenage, probably brought by travellers along the road or by terrified Londoners fleeing to the wholesome air of the country.

1381

The Peasants' Revolt against the Poll Tax and other injustices included men from Shephall who won temporary concessions from their lord of the manor, the Abbot of St Albans.

1446

The date of the earliest surving record of the Guild, Fraternity or Brotherhood of the Holy Trinity, whose members met regularly to say masses for the dead and for other religious and charitable purposes. They had their own Brotherhood House near the Bury Mead.

1506

Rector Stephen Hellard died and bequeathed a newly-built row of houses in Dead Lane (now Church Lane) to be used as almshouses 'for the habitation of three poor folk'. They continue to be used as such today.

11   Memorial brass to Rector Stephen Hellard.

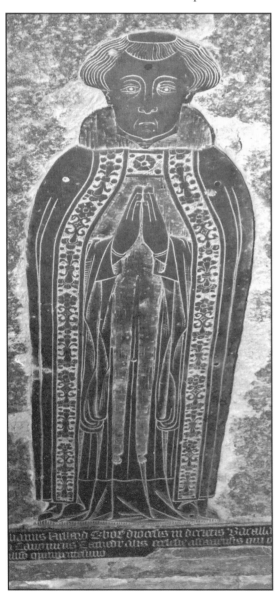

1530

The first surviving record of the *Swan Inn* (now The Grange) where a man named Maryott, who was accused of murder, died on 12 May.

1542

George Nodes bought the manor of Shephall which remained in the Nodes family until 1800.

1550

King Edward VI gave Stevenage to Nicholas Ridley, newly appointed Bishop of London.

1558

Rector Thomas Alleyne died, leaving provision in his will to establish a free grammar school in Stevenage.

1575

Stevenage Vestry records began. The Vestry was the forerunner of today's Borough Council and had responsibility for a number of local matters, such as providing for the poor.

1590

Richard Norwood, surveyor and explorer, was born at Cannix.

1640 - 1660

The English Civil War. St Nicholas' Church was despoiled.

April 1646

During the Civil War, King Charles I passed through Stevenage as he made his escape from Oxford where his army was besieged. He came via the old road from St Albans through Fishers Green. He was unrecognised, disguised as the servant of one of his own chaplains.

11 July 1647

The Parliamentary army marched King Charles through Stevenage from Royston, on their way to Hatfield House. Although a prisoner, he was frequently cheered along the route.

1649

After Cromwell's victory in the Civil War, lands formerly belonging to the Bishop of London were sold to private individuals. Stevenage was bought by Thomas Ayres.

1660

Following the Restoration of the monarchy, the Bishopric of London was re-established and Stevenage returned to its former lord of the manor, the Bishop of London. There was no further change until 1868, when such rights and duties as remained were transferred to the Ecclesiastical Commissioners, who still hold them today.

1664

Samuel Pepys recorded a visit to Stevenage in his diary, the first of many.

1676

Ten Stevenage people admitted publicly to being dissenters.

1690

Henry Boswell, King of the Gypsies, was born at Six Hills.

1720

The Stevenage and Biggleswade Turnpike Trust Act was passed in Parliament. About 60 local landowners, farmers and other investors became trustees, employing the necessary engineers and labourers to improve the road between Stevenage and Biggleswade. Other turnpike trusts were set up along the whole of what now became known as the Great North Road, bringing prosperity to the towns along its route, including Stevenage, which became famous as a great coaching town.

1724

Henry Trigg, owner of the *Old Castle* inn at the top of Middle Row, died leaving instructions in his will that the coffin containing his body was not to be buried but placed on the rafters in his barn. His intention was to avoid bodysnatchers, but this unusual feature made

the *Old Castle* a tourist attraction for the next two centuries. It also prevented the Stevenage Vestry from completing the agreement with Trigg to use his barn as the town's first workhouse. So the vestry negotiated instead with George Crouch, churchwarden, to use a building he owned and by the end of the year Stevenage's first workhouse was open, although too small from the start.

1737

A group of Quakers was registered as using Broomin Green Farm for religious worship.

1741

The first regular coach service to Stevenage was the 'Perseverance' which ran from Smithfield to Hitchin.

1756

Rector Nicholas Cholwell had the middle section of the ancient path from the High Street to St Nicholas' Church planted with lime and horse-chestnut trees, forming an avenue.

1765

The Pest Houses were built.

1773

The Stevenage Vestry bought John Hitchin's house opposite the pond and town lock-up at the south end of the High Street, for their new workhouse.

1778

Broadwater Farmhouse was built.

1790

John Wesley preached in Stevenage High Street.

1799

A Methodist chapel was opened in the High Street, in the building currently used as the Old Town Library.

1800

In the early years of the century at least one hundred coaches a day were passing through

12 The former workhouse (now Tudor House) in Letchmore Road, with the Stevenage Gas Company buildings on the right, *c.*1920-30.

Stevenage, bringing prosperity to the High Street's many inns, including the *New Inn* (later the *Coach and Horses*), the *Marquess of Lorne*, the *White Hart*, the *Fox* (later the *Unicorn*, now the Bombay Restaurant), the *Red Lion*, the *White Lion* and, most famous of all, known the length of the Great North Road, the *Swan* (now the Grange).

10 July 1807
Fire destroyed many of the buildings in the High Street between the *Swan Inn* and Middle Row. The old wooden buildings were subsequently rebuilt in brick.

29 September 1814
Nonconformist chapel opened in Stevenage, in connection with the Academy at Little Wymondley.

3 October 1829
Fire burned down the *White Hart Inn*, its stable of horses and 10 nearby buildings.

1833
The Stevenage Vestry bought a new, improved fire-engine, which was kept in its engine house attached to the almshouses in Back Lane (formerly Dead Lane, now Church Lane).

1 January 1834
The newly built National School (later known

as St Nicholas' School) opened on Bury Mead.

1835
Hitchin Union of Parishes formed. Stevenage no longer had its own workhouse.

1841
Extension to St Nicholas' Church built by Rector Blomfield.

1845
General Enclosure Act. Strips of land in the open fields in Stevenage were reallocated and fenced.

1846
The village school was built at Shephall.

1850
The Great Northern Railway station opened in Julian's Farm Road, after which road travel decreased rapidly and the High Street inns no longer flourished. New residents came to live in Stevenage, commuting to London by train. The population increased to 2,100 by mid-century.

1850
The *Swan Inn*, having been sold by its last landlord, Thomas Cass, to the Rev. John Osborne Seager, was converted to a boarding

13 London Road, *c*.1910. This part of the Great North Road ran from Six Hills to the High Street. A section of it remains today, behind the Leisure Centre.

14 *The Yorkshire Grey*, one of the coaching inns on the Great North Road, 1975.

FIRE
At Stevenage.

15 A notice requesting subscriptions to help those who lost property in the Stevenage fire of 1807.

THE number of Houses consumed by this fire, which broke out on the 10th, and again on the 12th of JULY, 1807, is Thirty-four, exclusive of Barns, Maltings, and other Out-Buildings, with very considerable Quantities of Corn, Hay, and other Stock too heavy to be removed, some Household Furniture and Working Tools.

An Estimate has been made of the loss with as much accuracy as the time and circumstances would admit, and care has been taken in every case not to exceed the Value of the Property destroyed.

	l.	s.	d.
The Amount of Buildings and Stock belonging to Persons wholly or in a great degree insured, and who are not in need of assistance	6171	6	0
The value of the Property of Persons less able to bear the loss is, exclusively of the Amount insured by them	1052	8	0
The Value of the Property of the same class of Persons insured	2025	10	0
The Value of Fourteen Cottages belonging to labouring Men and poor Widows not insured	1055	0	0
The Value of the Tools, Furniture, and Clothes of poor Persons destroyed	285	8	6
	£.10589	12	6

Property insured	7186	16	0
Ditto uninsured	3402	16	6
	10589	12	6

It is proposed by the Gentlemen at their Meeting the Relief of the Sufferers (considering the two last classes as the principal objects) to be under the direction of the Magistrates of the District, and a Committee of Subscribers,

SUBSCRIPTIONS WILL BE RECEIVED BY

Messrs. Hindley and Roe,	*Baldock.*
Mr. Bailey,	*Berkhamstead.*
Rev. Mr. Bargus,	*Barkway.*
Mr. Newton,	*Barnet.*
—— Drage,	*Buntingford.*
Rev. Mr. Armstrong,	*Cheshunt.*
Messrs. Mott and Times,	*Hadham.*
Rev. Mr. Thackeray,	*Hatfield.*
Mr. Grover,	*Hemel Hempstead.*
Messrs. Christie & Catherow,	*Hertford.*
Messrs. Wilshere & Co.	*Hitchin.*
Thomas Baskerfield, Esq.	*Redbourn.*
Stephen Salter, Esq.	*Rickmersworth.*
Messrs. Nash & Son,	*Royston.*
Messrs. Brabant & Co.	*St Albans.*
The Rev. the Minister	*Sawbridgeworth.*
Rev. Thomas Field,	*Stansted.*
Rev. Mr. Baker, } Mr. R. Whittington, }	*Stevenage.*
Messrs. Mortlock and Co.	*Stortford.*
Mr. Knight,	*Tring.*
Mr. King,	*Ware.*
Mr. George Whittingstall,	*Watford.*
Rev. Mr. Orde,	*Wheathamstead.*
Mr. Crawley,	*Welwyn.*
Messrs. Masterman & Co.	*White Hart Court, London.*

The Ministers of the different Parishes in this County, are requested to solicit Subscriptions, and to remit such as they may obtain, to any of the Persons above-mentioned.

A. MEETKERKE.
H. BAKER, *Rector of Stevenage.*

JOHN HILL,
D. CHAPMAN, } *Surveyors.*

J. BEDFORD, Printer, HITCHIN.

school and its name changed to the Grange.

1854

Albert Street was built, providing shops, modern houses, chapels and public houses.

1855

Stevenage Gas Company Ltd. was formed in the old workhouse.

1857

Police Constable Starkins was murdered and his body thrown into a pond at Norton Green.

Twins Albert Ebenezer and Ebenezer Albert Fox were born at Symonds Green.

1861

Holy Trinity Church was built at the south end of the town, on the site of the pond opposite the workhouse. Neighbouring farmers filled in the pond with cartloads of rubble. The parish lock-up was moved to the grounds of the workhouse. The straw-plait market continued on Saturday mornings in the open space between Holy Trinity Church, Southend farm and the High Street.

1865

Charles Dickens and Edward Bulwer Lytton opened the Guild of Literature and Arts building in London Road, near the Six Hills. They had devoted several years to raising the money for the project, which was intended to house impoverished writers and artists.

Unwin Unwin-Heathcote rebuilt Shephal-bury.

1 November 1868

Stevenage and Biggleswade Turnpike Trust was dissolved.

1871

The Town Hall was built in Railway Street (later renamed Orchard Road), with a new Police Station adjacent. As well as becoming the town's administrative centre, it also provided a venue for amateur dramatics and many social functions.

1872

Edward Gordon Craig was born to Ellen Terry at a house in Railway Street (now 23 Orchard Road).

The Saturday straw-plait market moved to the Town Hall and a small admission fee was charged.

1876

The Methodist Church was built on the corner of Sish Lane and London Road, on the site of former open-air meetings.

1883

The Educational Supply Association (ESA) opened their premises near the railway station, bringing employment opportunities to the town.

A Stevenage branch of the Church of England Temperance Society was formed.

1883 - 1893

Between the ages of four and fourteen E.M. Forster lived with his mother at Rooks Nest House, which became the inspiration for his novel *Howard's End*.

1885

Fresh water was piped to Stevenage from a borehole at Rooks Nest. Ironically, the Forsters living opposite were without even a well for most of their 10 years there.

William, son of the Reverend William Jowitt and his wife Louisa, was born at Stevenage Rectory. He later became Lord Chancellor of England.

1887

A second stretch of the Avenue was planted with limes and chestnuts to mark the Golden Jubilee of Queen Victoria. Trees were also planted along the High Street and London Road from the Bowling Green to Six Hills.

1894

The Local Government Act conferred the status of Urban District on Stevenage. The first Chairman of the Urban District Council was the Rector, William Jowitt.

1897

The Guild of Literature and Art was acknowledged a failure and sold.

1905

Composer Elizabeth Poston was born at Highfield.

1907

Clarence Elliott established a nursery for alpine plants at Six Hills.

1910

Letchmore Road Boys' school was opened by Hertfordshire County Council.

1916

New police station built in Stanmore Road.

1923

The railway loop line from Stevenage to Hertford was opened.

1927

Stevenage Knitting Company opened in Sish Lane.

   Vincent H.R.D. Company formed. It went on to build world famous motor bicycles.

1935

The third and final stretch of the Avenue, as far as Rectory Lane, was planted, in celebration of the Silver Jubilee of King George V.

1945

Death of self-made millionaire Jeremiah Inns. He left the bulk of his fortune for charitable purposes in Stevenage, including money to build almshouses in Inns Close. His former home, Springfield House, is now the Old Stevenage Community Centre. The first floor houses the Denington Gallery of the Stevenage Artists' Co-operative.

1945

William Jowitt, son of the former rector, became Lord Chancellor of England.

1946

Stevenage was designated Britain's first New Town.

20 May 1958

The new Stevenage coat of arms was adopted.

1962

The A1(M) bypass opened. The Great North road no longer ran through the town.

6 November 1975

Philip Ireton became the first Freeman of the Borough of Stevenage.

Chapter 2

Stevenage Neighbourhoods

The present boundaries of the Borough of Stevenage include all the hamlets, greens and manors which have for centuries formed the parish of Stevenage, together with the previously quite separate villages of Shephall and Broadwater. Many of these ancient settlements, often inhabited by only a handful of people, have given their names to the modern 'neighbourhoods' and seen their populations increase by factors of thousands in the 50 years since Stevenage was designated a New Town.

Explaining the neighbourhood concept in their 1949 publication *The New Town of Stevenage*, a Development Corporation official wrote.

> The present town of Stevenage is itself to be the nucleus of the first neighbourhood of the New Town. There will be added in due course ... five other neighbourhoods which will be called by the names of existing hamlets and farms; Bedwell, Broadwater, Shephall, Chells and Pin Green. On average, about ten thousand people will live in each of these neighbourhoods.

16   St Mary's Church, Shephall, *c*.1920.

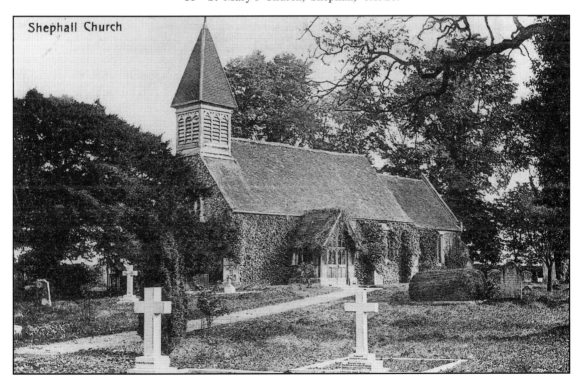

Shephall Church

The original plan was to develop a New Town of 60,000 people, which would have been six times the existing population, but since those early days there has been increased expansion to the present population of 80,000. To the six neighbourhoods at first envisaged have been added the enormous housing estates at Symonds Green, The Poplars and Chells Manor Village, with more to follow at Wellfield Wood.

The pioneer planners of Stevenage, Britain's first New Town, had visions of town and country combining harmoniously to give the best of both worlds.

> The new Stevenage will comprise an area of about six thousand acres. The existing town of about 6,500 people covers only a fraction of it, the rest being farmland and woodland. By no means all of this will be built over. The woods and copses will be preserved, so will the vast majority of single trees and many of the existing hedgelines ... The north Hertfordshire landscape is a rolling landscape of peculiar charm, with spacious fields, tall ashes and elms. Not only will New Town dwellers be able to take their country walks through it but by the skill of the landscape architect something of the character of the local countryside will pervade the whole of the town itself.

Perhaps the planners genuinely did not understand that preserving individual trees and hedges, even woods and copses cannot encapsulate 'the character of the local countryside' if the rural way of life that depended on that countryside is destroyed, as it inevitably must be when farmland and open country is built upon. Yet it is still possible to trace the old lanes and footpaths that linked Stevenage to Shephall by way of Whomerley Wood, or the ancient trackway, used by Roman invaders and the fugitive King Charles I, which passes through Symonds Green and Fishers Green, or the historic Great North Road from London, which ran past the *Roebuck Inn* at Broadwater and straight on beside the Six Hills before broadening out into Stevenage High Street.

Those who remember the Stevenage district as it was, have no difficulty now in forgetting the modern buildings and roads and seeing again Cuckoo Wood, Trinity Road, Sishes, Highfield, Bedwell Plash and the Six Hills in all their splendid isolation on the east side of the Great North Road. For those who never knew this countryside there are clues in the names of modern streets, in a scrap of hedgerow, or in a tidied up and asphalted pathway which once ran beside cornfields.

In 1957 a competition was announced for the design of a coat of arms for the town. A Barclay School pupil won with a superb design combining elements from the past, present and planned future of Stevenage. On 20 May 1958 it was officially adopted by the Stevenage Urban District Council at a ceremony in the Town Hall in Orchard Road, in the presence of Councillors G. Balderstone, C. Carey, S. Clark, J. Cockerton, M. Cotter, K. Ellis, S. Ellis, J. Grice, F. Hide, P. Ireton, A.C. Luhman, S. Munden, F. Newberry, F. Udell, H. Warren (chairman) and retiring councillors Mrs. K. Newman and L. Smith. The design features an oak tree, the sword of the Bishops of London, the Great North Road and six stars, representing the six neighbourhoods; Old Stevenage, Bedwell, Broadwater, Chells, Pin Green and Shephall.

The Ordnance Survey of 1946, and all earlier maps, show Stevenage and Shephall as two quite separate entities, each with its own church. Some of the other settlements within what is now Stevenage had their own churches in the distant past, but by the middle ages most had fallen into disuse as their tiny populations were even further depleted after the Black Death in the 14th century. It was the decision to move down the hill to the main road that saved the population of Stevenage from a similar decline, enabling it to profit through trade and to develop into a town with a large enough population to survive epidemics.

Shephall, always smaller than Stevenage, also survived, but never grew beyond a village. It was recorded in Domesday Book as having sufficient woodland for 20 pigs and land for four ploughs, compared with Stevenage's 50 pigs and seven ploughs. At this time Shephall had two landlords, Lanfranc, Archbishop of Canterbury, who held two hides (one hide is

17 The Stevenage Borough coat of arms.

about 120 acres) and the Abbot of St Albans, who held three hides. By the end of the 11th century the Abbot of St Albans had managed to acquire the Archbishop's two hides and Shephall became entirely the property of St Albans Abbey, an association which was to continue for nearly 800 years.

Under the Saxon manorial system of government, counties were divided into 'hundreds' for administrative purposes, each hundred having its own court. Stevenage, Knebworth, Welwyn, Hatfield and neighbouring towns and villages were in the Hundred of Broadwater. However, from the end of the 11th century Shephall became a detached parish of the Hundred of Cassio, because it belonged to St Albans, which was in Cassio Hundred. This arrangement was not unique, but it may have seemed a little odd to the people of Broadwater and Shephall, whose villages adjoined.

It is known that there was a church in Shephall in 1151 because in that year the Prior of Reading Abbey, which had hitherto administered the Shephall church, agreed to transfer it to St Albans Abbey in return for an annual payment of a silver half mark and the transfer of another church from St Albans to Reading. In common with most churches of this period, St Mary's, Shephall was probably a wooden structure, subsequently rebuilt of flint and stone in the next centuries.

Shephall church possesses two very interesting bells which are still rung today. One is the oldest church bell in Hertfordshire and is at least 800 years old, having been made in the late 12th century. The other, a mere youngster, is dated 1767. Both bells were rehung by the Whitechapel Foundry in 1974. A more recent restoration was the complete replacement of the weathervane and its supports, together with the regilding of its finials. The money for this project was raised through the publication of the history of Shephall, entitled *Tyme out of mind* in 1984. The author, Mary Spicer, was born in Shephall and spent many years researching the history of the village.

The late 14th century was a time of discontent among the peasant farmers and townsfolk of England. Landlords were demanding ever higher rents and showing no leniency to those in difficulty. A further imposition came in the reign of King Richard II, when a poll tax was imposed. For many in Hertfordshire this was the last straw and in 1381 they joined forces with the men of Kent and Essex to march on London. At the same time, the people of Shephall joined the townsfolk of St Albans to demand certain rights from the Abbot. Along with some other villages, they were successful and returned to Shephall bearing a list of concessions. Their triumph was short-lived. Within a month, King Richard II came in person to St Albans and decreed all concessions granted by the Abbot null and void. He then ordered the men of Hertfordshire to St Albans, where they swore an oath of allegiance to him.

When King Henry VIII dissolved the monasteries and disposed of their lands,

Shephall was sold, in 1542, to George Nodes, one of the king's Sergeants of Buckhounds. He paid £197 14s. 8d. for the manor of Shephall, which then remained in the Nodes family until 1800.

For most of the 19th century the Heathcote family were lords of the manor of Shephall. They were of a different calibre from the Nodes, wealthy, eccentric and reactionary. Samuel Unwin-Heathcote is recorded in the 1840s as being against Catholic emancipation, parliamentary reform, the Corn Laws and the railways. He was particularly vehement about the latter and was prosecuted for obstructing the building of the Great Northern Railway as it crossed his land. He may have been aware that an earlier proposal had been to route the railway from Welwyn via Kimpton to Hitchin, thus avoiding Stevenage altogether. Annoyingly for him, it was opposition from local landowners that forced the company to build the existing route.

In 1865 Unwin Unwin-Heathcote, son of Samuel, pulled down the old Shephalbury and rebuilt it in ornate gothic style. It later became known as Shephall manor.

The Heathcotes also donated land and money for the building of a school at Shephall, to enable the village children to be taught in purpose-built accommodation instead of in the small, inconvenient cottage that had been used previously. The new school, built by Bates and Warren of Stevenage, was opened in 1846.

It was a member of the Heathcote family, Miss Evelyn Heathcote, the oldest inhabitant of the village, who planted the Silver Jubilee oak on the village green in 1935, at a ceremony to celebrate 25 years of King George V's reign. The village at this time had a population of about 200, most people were employed in work connected with the land and, to a large extent, it was still remote from urban life, even though, as the crow flies, so near the Great North Road and the Great Northern Railway. But for most village people, walking was their usual means of transport and they used the field paths to Stevenage for their shopping, entertainment and other needs.

After St Mary's Church, the oldest building in Shephall is the *Red Lion*, which was in existence at least as far back as the early 18th

18   Shephalbury, *c*.1919. Threatened with demolition in the 1990s, it was saved by a well organised campaign on the part of local residents.

19 The *Roebuck Inn* in the 19th century.

century, although it was not known by that name until later. Although now modernised and extended, the *Red Lion* retains some of its original structure, the historic ambience helped by the copies of old deeds which decorate its walls.

From Shephall village, footpaths led in all directions, although some were diverted by the Heathcotes from the traditional rights of way that crossed their land. About one mile to the east, at the fork of the Great North Road and the Hertford-Stevenage road, is the hamlet of Broadwater. By the 20th century it consisted only of a few cottages, a blacksmith's shop, the *Roebuck Inn* and Broadwater Farmhouse, but at one time it had been a place of importance, giving its name to the Hundred of Broadwater. The Stevenage Brook which flows through it on its way to the River Beane used to become swollen with water draining down from higher ground at this point, spreading out across marshy land marked on old Ordnance Survey maps as 'Liable to Flood.'

It is difficult now to estimate the significance of this place to people some 1500 years ago, when the system of Hundreds was devised. In recent centuries Broadwater has been a tiny hamlet associated with Shephall, giving no visible indication of its former importance. A single Saxon hut excavated in 1961 in Broadwater Crescent did not throw much more light on this subject, as there is no way of knowing its function, whether it was part of an isolated settlement or a sizeable village.

Broadwater Farmhouse has recently been restored for commercial purposes, after years left unoccupied. It was built in 1778 for Richard Whittington, formerly innkeeper at the *Swan* in Stevenage High Street. He was apparently an excellent farmer, employing up-to-date methods when appropriate, but following traditional ploughing techniques with wooden ploughs drawn by teams of oxen. He grew turnips, swedes, barley, clover, wheat, peas and oats on the 950 acres that comprised Broadwater farm and neighbouring Half Hyde Farm.

The *Roebuck Inn*, standing at the fork of two major roads, benefited from the activities of both the Stevenage and Biggleswade

Turnpike Trust and the Watton Trust. As the roads were improved, they attracted stage coaches, mail coaches and much other traffic—including highwaymen and other unsavoury characters. Among the many myths associated with the name of Dick Turpin is one that claims he used to escape pursuit through an underground tunnel leading from the *Roebuck*. He is also said to have hidden in a secret passage in the *Swan*, in the High Street. Since his supposed non-stop ride from London to York has been disproved by historians—the ride was actually carried out by William Nevison—it is possible that these other stories may also be shown to be figments of the imagination. Meanwhile, they are happily kept alive for future generations in the road name Turpin's Rise.

During the 19th and early 20th centuries the *Roebuck* was a favourite meeting place for local hunts, who would gather outside before setting off for a day's sport. On one occasion they were joined by the Prince of Wales, who abdicated the throne of England in 1935 before he could be crowned King Edward VIII.

Field paths from Shephall to Stevenage led past Whomerley Wood and adjoining Monks' Wood. The irrational modern spelling of 'Whomerley' has naturally confused newcomers to Stevenage. The correct, age-old pronunciation is 'Humley.' In addition to the word of those remaining residents who were here before the New Town was built, there is ample written evidence of the way the name should be pronounced. Medieval documents record the family of Homle or Homlie. Early maps use variations of 'Humlie' and 'Humley' and the first Ordnance Survey map used the form 'Omlie.' Many local people used to call it 'Humbly Wood' and reports in some late 19th-century editions of the *Hertfordshire Express* newspaper also use this form.

Records show that there were settlements in Whomerley Wood at least at the time of the Norman Conquest and probably before. The earthworks which are still visible there are the remains of a homestead surrounded by a moat. Ivo de Homle held land in

Stevenage in 1275 and Ralph de Homle in 1293.

From Whomerley Wood, the ancient path continued through fields thick with wheat, poppies and cornflowers in summer, or ploughed furrows glinting with flintstones in winter, to Bedwell Plash. Here was a spring which fed a streamlet and a marshy pond, where rushes and flag irises grew. It has now been neatened and extended to make the Town Centre lake. The old black weatherboarded farm barns made a perfect background on a frosty day for sparkling white spiders' webs and Bedwell Lane itself, leading down to the Great North Road, was lined on one side with red-berried holly bushes. Among the houses and gardens opposite was that belonging to Clarence Elliott, the Six Hills nurseryman.

Walter Bedwell, who died in 1536, may well have lived here. His will implies that he was a widower of some wealth. He made careful provision for his young sons to be looked after by their older sisters. Among the goods he left to his daughter Alice were, 'my wife's best gown, a coverlet next the best, a mattress with the worst bolster and the best pillow.'

One of the older established neighbourhoods of the New Town is Chells. It has doubled in size in recent years since the building of Chells Manor Village pushed the Stevenage Borough boundary further east. For many centuries Chells consisted only of a farm and cottages centred round the timber-framed manor house. At the time of the Domesday Survey it was closely associated with Box, an almost contiguous village on the road to Walkern. The two settlements shared a church sited in a clearing in Box Wood, but this was in ruins by 1530 and had vanished from sight by 1728. Subsequently Box became part of Walkern parish and Chells part of Stevenage.

The name Chells originated as *Escelveia* or *Scelve* probably meaning Ash-tree-slope, but historian Henry Chauncy had another interpretation. In his *Historical Antiquities of Hertfordshire* published in 1700, he wrote of 'this manor of Cheles, so termed from a chil, a cold place.'

Stevenage is surrounded by greens, two of which, Pin Green and Symonds Green, have given their names to modern neighbourhoods. Pin Green, at one of the highest points in Stevenage, was designated by the New Town planners as the appropriate site for water reservoirs to be constructed 'from which most of the town will be supplied by gravity.' A 90-ft. high water tower was also built to supply water to those buildings for which a gravity feed was not possible.

The name Pin Green originated in the middle ages as 'Pynd' or 'Pound' Green where stray animals were kept. Nearby was the house called Sishes, probable home of the Sish family. John Sish was one of the 12 men charged with the responsibility of collecting information for the survey of land and property entitled *Stevenage Inventory and Terrier* in 1315. In the late 19th century the house was occupied by Julius Bertram, M.P., lawyer, musician and patron of the arts. Nearby was Highfield, a substantial mansion owned in the 1880s by Mr. Salmon, from 1886 to 1914 by the Postons and subsequently by the Keysell family.

A tragedy occurred here in 1884 when Mr. Salmon's coachman, Mr. Camplin, hanged himself from a beam in a barn at Highfield, shortly before he was due to be married to a Mrs. Lovegrove. The local paper reported that he was about 60 years of age and had 'lately taken to intemperate habits.'

Sishes was also in the 19th century the site of the Stevenage Cottage Hospital. In 1882 Annie Sharp of Norton Green contracted scarlet fever while working as a servant at Hitchin and Dr. Hill Smith arranged for her to be admitted to the Cottage Hospital, where she was nursed back to health. Pin Green also had its public house, the *Three Horseshoes*, on the Walkern Road, which was in existence at least as far back as 1773. In that year there was a complaint against William Spencer, the licensee, for 'harbouring people on Sundays'. All these buildings at Pin Green were destroyed during the development of the New Town.

About half a mile north of Pin Green is the hamlet of Rooks Nest, notable as the site of Stevenage's first fresh water supply from the borehole opened there in 1885 and as the childhood home of novelist E.M. Forster. He

20 Gleaners in the fields at Pin Green in 1788.

and his widowed mother lived at Rooks Nest House from 1883 to 1893. Ironically, the borehole only a few yards across the road did not benefit them; for most of their time at Rooks Nest they did not even possess a well, but had to buy their drinking water from the Franklins at Rooks Nest farm next door.

The remaining Stevenage greens are on the west side of the railway line which effectively cut Stevenage in two when it was opened in 1850. Fishers Green is the site of some of the earliest evidence of human activity in the Stevenage district. Flints and Old Stone Age implements have been found here and the remains of the ancient track from Verulamium to Baldock is still used as a footpath to Corey's Mill.

For most of the 19th century the buildings clustered round the Green were the *Fisherman Inn*, Stebbing Farm, owned by George Moules,

and some cottages. The only source of drinking water for the cottage dwellers was a pond, about which there were frequent complaints, often brushed aside by the Medical Officer of Health who stated that the people seemed healthy enough. In fact, some rural cottage dwellers here and elsewhere in the district lived wretched lives in insanitary conditions, cut off from the mainstream of life in the town. The parish church made attempts to improve their lives by setting up meeting rooms in outlying districts, such as the one in a cottage at Fishers Green, where religious services, basic lessons in housecraft and social gatherings were held.

A dramatic increase in the population of Fishers Green occurred in the 1890s, following the establishment of the ESA factory near the station. A small housing development took place along Fishers Green Road with the

21   The entrance drive to Highfield, birthplace of Elizabeth Poston, photographed in 1913.

22 Harvesting at Langmoor Farm, Symonds Green, in the 1930s.

building of Jubilee, Huntingdon, Bournemouth and Southsea Roads. A general store was opened on the corner of Huntingdon road by the Scarborough family. With remarkable foresight local people nicknamed this area 'New Town' and even ran their own football club, 'Newtown Rovers', little knowing that the future would bring a real New Town, and that an enormous road, with a population equal to the whole of 19th-century Stevenage, would be named after the Scarboroughs' shop.

Symonds Green, now so densely populated, was previously even smaller and more picturesque than Fishers Green, consisting only of a few cottages and the *Crooked Billet* public house beside the pond. Apart from the attractiveness of the place, its only claim to fame was as the birthplace in 1857 of the twin poachers, Albert and Ebenezer Fox, whose father Henry farmed ten acres of land. He

rented his cottage on the green firstly from Sarah Moules, then from Thomas Franklin.

Adjoining Symonds Green, and remembered today in the name of Woolenwick School, was the manor of Woolenwick. According to Domesday Book, it was very tiny and already in decline in 1086. No ploughs were recorded, although it did have some meadowland, perhaps more than other parts of Stevenage. This may be the origin of the surviving road name of Meadway and of the Oakmead Nurseries where cucumbers, tomatoes, chrysanthemums and other glasshouse crops were grown in the 1940s and '50s. They are now under concrete. Since the Domesday Survey, no surviving record of Woolenwick has been found.

A little further south lay Broomin Green, once known as Cannix. Broomin Green Farmhouse still survives, surrounded by factory buildings, in the angle of Fairlands Way and Fairview Road. The existing farmhouse is of 17th-century origin, but there may well have been an earlier building on the same site. John Chertsey, of Broxbourne, often referred to as John de Broxbourne, was lord of the manor of Cannix in 1308. The pioneering surveyor and explorer, Richard Norwood, was born at Cannix in 1590.

On 10 January 1737-8 a group of Quakers registered their intention to meet for religious worship at the house of Thomas Impey and Dennis Crown at Broomin Green. During the Second World War the first German bombs to be dropped on Stevenage fell at Broomin Green, no doubt aimed at the railway line. The farmhouse remained intact, and was subsequently bought by Camford Engineering and used for business meetings. The Hooper family who lived there during the late 1970s, when Mrs. Hooper was resident housekeeper, had reason to believe it haunted, after experiencing doorbells ringing of their own accord and hearing footsteps moving across the empty first-floor landing towards a bricked-up door.

In the extreme south east of the Stevenage Borough boundary, on the edge of the Knebworth House estate, is Norton Green. Always a remote hamlet, it has been divided ever more firmly from both Old and New Stevenage, first by the Great Northern Railway and more recently by the A1 motorway. To arrive there today it is necessary to traverse the expanse of the Gunnels Wood industrial area and seek out, behind the brightly lit factories, the narrow lane that plunges suddenly between high hedges leading, it seems, into the rural past.

Clustered together facing the pond are *The Woodman* public house, a row of traditional Hertfordshire flint cottages, a close of modern houses and Norton Green Farm. Beyond, the road becomes a muddy track leading past the hornbeams and hazels of Watery Grove deep into Newton Wood and on to the woodyard at Pigeons' Wick. Woodland flowers, birds and deer abound at Watery Grove which, for a number of years, was leased to the Hertfordshire and Middlesex Trust for Nature Conservation as a nature reserve.

Norton Green has known tragedy and violence. In 1857 the mutilated body of Police Constable John Starkins was found in a pond nearby and Jeremiah Carpenter, a labourer employed by Mr. Horn of Norton Green Farm, was tried for the murder and acquitted, in a case that was never satisfactorily resolved.

As at Fishers Green, the Church attempted to reach out to the isolated cottage dwellers at Norton Green by setting up in the late 19th century a small mission hut there for services and social gatherings. For many years after the Great Northern Railway line was opened, the only means of getting from one side to the other was by foot crossings. Children living at Norton Green and attending school in Stevenage had to face deadly danger twice a day and on 24 November 1886 the inevitable happened. Hannah and George Marvel of Wilmore Common, Norton Green, were killed by an express train as they crossed the line in thick fog. In spite of this it was not until Chequers Bridge Road was built that a road bridge over the railway made crossing safe.

Chapter 3

The Great North Road

The road that shaped the history of Stevenage began as one of a series of prehistoric tracks leading somewhat disjointedly from what is now London, to the north. In Roman times parts of it, including the Stevenage section from Broadwater through what is now the High Street, were straightened, properly surfaced and drained to create a continuous road from Cripplegate to York.

However there were many other routes to and from London, both ancient tracks and well-constructed Roman roads. For many centuries during and after the Roman occupation the main road from London to the north ran some miles to the east of Stevenage, passing through Ware and Royston. This was Ermine Street, later known as the North Road, then as the Old North Road or A10. It was not until after the turnpike trusts were set up in the 18th century that the reconstructed road from London via Barnet, Welwyn, Stevenage and Baldock became the major route to the north, known as the Great North Road.

For the inhabitants of Stevenage, the road had been inextricably bound up with their lives from the time that the village moved down from its original hilltop site. Predominantly a farming community until after the Second World War, they relied upon the road for transporting their produce to London. It is tempting to imagine an idyllic rural scene of horse-drawn wagons, loaded with grain and vegetables, moving slowly through the High Street on their way south. The return journey was not so attractive, as reeking cartloads of manure and refuse were brought back from

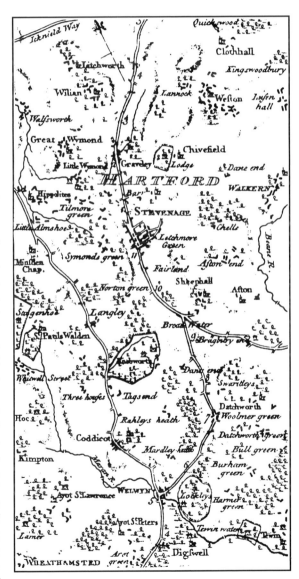

23 Map of the Great North Road in the 18th century.

25

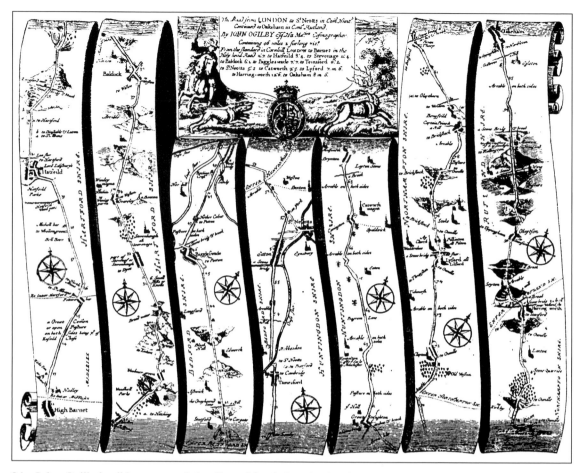

24 John Ogilby's ribbon map of the Great North Road, showing Broadwater, Six Hills and Stevenage.

London for the very necessary purpose of fertilising the fields.

From its early beginnings until the early 20th century much of the High Street consisted of working farm houses, with yards immediately behind them and fields beyond. The High Street resounded to the bellowing of cattle, cocks crowing at dawn and the clucking of chickens as they scrabbled about in the back yards or out in the road. Dogs roamed freely and it was no rare occurrence for cattle, donkeys and other animals to escape their pens and wander into the High Street. For most of the time the pace of life, geared as it was to the slow-moving wagons, was such that no harm was done. The occasional irresponsible horse-rider would gallop through, endangering children and the elderly,

and sometimes a bull would break loose, causing bystanders to move swiftly indoors.

During the 17th, 18th and early 19th centuries cattle drovers from the north who brought their beasts down to London regularly stopped at Stevenage where they found refreshment for themselves and their animals. The open space around the market cross at the top of Middle Row was the site of the cattle market. There were several ponds in the High Street, one near the Bowling Green, one outside the *White Lion* and a watery complex at the south end, all of which were linked by a rivulet running the length of the street, making it very suitable for cattle. Townspeople were tempted to empty their refuse into it, adding further aromas to those emanating from the cattle. To reduce the hazards of crossing such a filthy road, little footbridges were built over the stream.

So great was the weight of traffic on major roads that by the end of the 17th century most were in a very poor state. The standards of road building and upkeep established by the Romans had long since been abandoned. To make matters worse, the system of 'statute labour', which had been made law in the 16th century, requiring each parish to be responsible for the upkeep of roads within its boundaries, could not cope with the amount of maintenance required. Towns such as Stevenage, whose roads were in constant use, suffered heavy demands in this respect although, of course, their inhabitants benefited from the trade engendered by the road.

In addition to the inevitable problems created by the volume of traffic, there was also the selfish behaviour of certain local residents to contend with. Assize Court records for 1602 state that, on 12 July that year, Francis Godfrey narrowed and obstructed 'the highway from London to Stevenage at Burleigh Bottom [near Knebworth] ... by digging a pond or pit there'. Over the centuries many of those who lived beside a road succumbed to the temptation of extending their property by taking over a piece of the common highway.

The road between Stevenage and Graveley was a cause of concern to the inhabitants of Stevenage in 1683, when they were taken to court for failing to repair 'a certain highway leading from Graveley to Stevenage, 200 poles in length'. They got little help from Graveley man George Hampton who, the following year, was accused of 'stopping up a water-course in Graveley parish and turning of it into a highway between Graveley and Stevenage'. Eventually the necessary repairs were carried out and on 27 April 1685 J.P.s Sir William Lytton and Sir Charles Cleaver were able to issue the Stevenage authorities with a certificate 'of the good repair of the highway leading from Graveley to Stevenage'.

The road brought other visitors besides the traders, cattle-drovers, pilgrims and travellers who were so beneficial to the Stevenage economy. Disease came with those fleeing the Black Death in the 14th century and the plague outbreaks, culminating in the Great Plague of London, in 1665. The diarist, Samuel Pepys, who escaped the plague, came frequently to Stevenage during the 1660s, often putting up at the *Swan Inn* on his way to and from his parents' home at Brampton in Huntingdonshire. On 5 August 1664 he stayed the night at the *Swan*, awaiting the arrival of his wife in a coach from Biggleswade. Next morning he played 'a game of bowls on the green there—till 8 o'clock

25 Six Hills, looking north, *c*.1950. A car can be seen on the Great North Road, to the left.

and then comes my wife in the coach, and a coach full of women. So, very joyful, drank there ...'.

Stevenage was fortunate in that no Civil War battle was fought in its vicinity, although there was serious fighting all around, at Barnet, St Albans and Hertford. However, during this and other wars, troops marched through the town, the less disciplined ranks sometimes stopping to steal, rape or destroy. No doubt local people breathed sighs of relief when they had gone, whichever cause they supported.

Robbers of other kinds also frequented the road; footpads, pickpockets and highwaymen. One, James Whitney, is thought to have been a local man, possibly born illegitimate and taking his name from Whitney Wood. There are conflicting opinions about him. Some people believed from his manner and his fine clothes that he was a gentleman, others that

26 Highwayman James Whitney in prison at Newgate in 1693.

he was a former butcher's boy, utterly cruel and lacking in compassion. A ballad telling his life story in ten verses may have been written by Whitney himself when he was in Newgate Gaol, where he was executed on 1 February 1693. The name of Robbery Bottom Lane, near Welwyn, commemorates the activities of highwaymen such as Whitney, who frequented this stretch of road. How fortunate for Samuel Pepys that their paths did not cross on the night of 11 October 1667, when he arrived at the *Swan* with a basket of gold which he hid under the bed, after a nervous journey on the coach from Brampton.

Tradition has it that Dick Turpin, who lived from 1706-39, stayed often at the *Swan*, escaping capture by hiding in a secret passage. There is no doubt of the existence of the passage, which was blocked up shortly after the Second World War when children from the Briar Patch Home were living at the Grange, as it was called by then.

Another diarist who travelled the road through Stevenage to Biggleswade in the 1720s was Daniel Defoe. He wrote, 'This indeed is a most frightful way', but he was glad to know that measures were in hand to improve it. No doubt he was referring to the Stevenage and Biggleswade Turnpike Trust, which had been established in 1720 by Act of Parliament. Similar trusts were being set up throughout the country, with groups of investors, often local landowners, putting money into improving and maintaining their stretch of road in the hope of making a profit from tolls levied on travellers.

As all the major roads were turnpiked, the various sections of a route, each managed by a separate Trust, became joined to form continuous highways. Thus the Great North Road came into being. Tollgates, or turnpike gates, were set up at strategic points along the roads, manned by a keeper who often lived in a purpose-built cottage beside it. All road users were charged, on a sliding scale. The Stevenage and Biggleswade Turnpike Trust had the following categories of user; 6-horse coaches or chaises; 4-horse coaches or chaises; 3- and 2-horse coaches or chaises; 1-horse

27 Milestone of the Stevenage and Biggleswade Turnpike Trust, still in position south of the *Granby Inn*.

28 Horace Allison's saddlery, seen here, above right, in the 1950s, was situated next door to the *Red Lion* in the High Street.

coaches, chaises or carts; 9ft. wagons or carts, charged per horse; 6 ft. wagons or carts, charged per horse; NW wagons or carts, charged per horse; horses, mules and asses; oxen or meat cattle; hogs, sheep or lambs.

Stevenage had a turnpike just north of the *Marquess of Granby Inn*. Inevitably, some travellers found ways of evading the toll charges, by entering or leaving the turnpike road on a side road such as Corey's Mill Lane. The Trustees noted at their meeting in the *White Horse*, Baldock, on 9 March 1733: 'Complaint having been made to this committee that several carriages ... do frequently avoid paying at the Stevenage Turnpike by going out of this road'. As a result, the turnpike gate was moved to Graveley in 1734, but was moved back again after six months, when a more effective deterrent was

found to be the setting up of side gates in Corey's Mill Lane and Holt Lane, Graveley.

Each Trust had the right to take road mending materials such as gravel and flints from private land, provided that compensation was paid. They also had powers of compulsory purchase if they deemed it necessary to widen or divert a road. At a meeting on 30 August 1745 the Trustees 'ordered that the treasurer do pay to Mr. Benjamin Lawrence two pounds six shillings and six pence for 20 poles of land near Stevenage Turnpike where a gravel pit has been lately opened'.

The traditional practice of repairing roads by statute labour still continued after the turnpike trusts came into being. This meant that a trust was able to take over the right previously held by parish vestries of calling on major householders to provide men, horses

29 The Heaney family outside the *Marquess of Lorne*, *c*.1920. Left to right: John Heaney, his parents Alice and Jack Heaney, and his wife Annie.

30 Advertisement for the *Marquess of Lorne*, *c*.1935.

and tools to repair the road for a certain number of days each year. The following notice was issued on 29 November 1796 to the Graveley labourers who were to carry out the work:

> Take notice. You are hereby required to attend and do duty on the Stevenage and Biggleswade Turnpike Road ... on Monday, Tuesday and Wednesday in the next week and to meet at the blacksmith's shop in Graveley at six o'clock in the morning.

> L. Trustram, Surveyor.

The practice of statute labour continued into the next century. On 29 October 1813, Justices of the Peace Adolphus Meetherke, who was also surveyor to the Trust, and the Rector, the Rev. Henry Baker, issued a list of people required to provide labourers to undertake road repairs, stating the number of days due from each:

Mary Cass	— 30 days	
John Smith	— 15 days	with one
Edward Parkins, Esq.	— 10 days	team and
George Newman	— 8 days	one able
Thomas Stalley	— 7 days	man each
William Stratton	— 5 days	

The improvement brought about by the turnpike trusts was responsible for an enormous increase in road travel, which in turn was a source of profit for tradesmen such as innkeepers, blacksmiths, coach owners, horse-breeders and brewers. Stevenage became an important coaching town. The first regular coach service recorded as passing through was the 'Perseverance', which continued for 100 years, from 1741, bringing passengers from the *Greyhound Inn* at Smithfield to the *Sun* at Hitchin, later continuing to Bedford. By 1800 some 20 coaches entered Stevenage every day, including mail coaches. They did not always arrive safely. On 1 March 1810, mail bags containing letters for delivery to Hatfield, Welwyn, Stevenage and other places along the Great North Road were stolen in London. The Postmaster put out notices offering £100 reward for information leading to a conviction but, as far as is known, without success.

Once Stevenage became established as a coaching town its fame spread and a highly romanticised picture of it remained in the general memory for many years. The historian, Herbert Tompkins, compiling his *Highways and Byways in Hertfordshire*, wrote in 1902, 'I come out at length upon the Great North Road eager for further journeying ... on the very edge of one of the famous coaching roads in old England ...'. He went on to describe the migration of medieval Stevenage to the road and its subsequent destruction by fire, following which,

> ... a new town was gradually built to the south west on either side of the Great North Road. And the town was just such an one as is dear to the heart of Englishmen—a town where all sorts and conditions of men lived almost within a few yards of one another, a town through which the coach rattled merrily on its way from the *Greyhound Inn* at Smith-field ...
> The *White Lion* is said to be the oldest inn in Stevenage, the *Baldock*, the *Boston*, the York *High-Flyer* and other coaches drew up before its door to change their teams; the wisdom and the wit of Stevenage were exercised in its largest room ...

In fact, when coaches drew up before the door of the *White Lion* they did so because its archway was too low to allow a stage-coach to pass beneath it. Passengers had to alight in the open space beside the inn, but this minor inconvenience does not seem to have detracted from its position as a coaching inn and the main meeting place for the town.

At the height of the coaching era, Stevenage High Street was full of noise and activity. Rival coaches tried to outdo each other in speed, requiring innkeepers to have teams of horses ready to change the instant a coach arrived. The *Swan* had a particularly good reputation as a coaching inn, maintaining extra stabling in a thatched building behind the Bowling Green. It was also recommended by discerning travellers along the Great North Road for its remarkable landlord, Thomas Cass, a learned man who enjoyed conversing with educated guests in Latin and Greek and maintained an unusually cultured and convivial establishment.

31 Stevenage High Street in the 1930s. The *White Lion*, on the left, is advertising garage services.

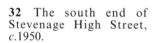

32 The south end of Stevenage High Street, *c*.1950.

33 The bus stop in the High Street seen here *c*.1950, was opposite the *White Lion*. The white building on the right was the clinic, next to the *Cromwell Hotel*.

The Great Northern railway opened its Stevenage station in 1850, putting an end to the coaching era. Stevenage High Street declined from being the colourful resort of travellers to a street which Charles Dickens, looking out from the window of the *White Hart*, described in 1861 as 'wide for its height, silent for its size and drowsy in the dullest degree ...'. Inns began closing their doors and turning into private houses. Thomas Cass sold the *Swan* to the Rev. John Osborne Seager, a curate and master at Alleyne's School, who changed its name to the Grange and converted it to a boarding school. The road itself was no longer kept up by the Stevenage and Biggleswade Turnpike Trust which, like most of the other trusts, had not made a profit. Roads became the responsibility of the local highway boards in 1862, although the life of the Stevenage Trust was extended annually from 1863 until its termination on 1 November 1868.

Perhaps the lack of coach traffic made the Local Board a little neglectful, since by the end of the century the High Street was poorly surfaced, thick mud in winter and dusty in summer. Describing Charles Wilcox's progress along it in an early motor car, E.M. Forster wrote in *Howard's End*:

> ... he turned round in his seat, and contemplated the cloud of dust that they had raised in their passage through the village. It was settling again, but not all into the road from which he had taken it. Some of it had percolated through the open windows, some had whitened the roses and gooseberries of the wayside gardens, while a certain proportion had entered the lungs of the villagers. 'I wonder when they'll learn wisdom and tar the roads,' was his comment.

If the railway emptied the road of coaches, it brought newcomers to live in Stevenage. Attracted by the ease of rail travel to London, people began moving into new houses along the London Road—that part of the Great North Road between Sish Lane and Six Hills—into Fairview Road, built in 1906 by the Great Northern Railway Company and originally called New Road, and into Julian's Road, Essex Road and the other roads that were springing up near the station.

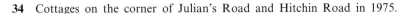

34 Cottages on the corner of Julian's Road and Hitchin Road in 1975.

Cromwell Hotel

Stevenage :: Herts

A.A.   ✿   R.A.C.

FULLY LICENSED
H. & C. RUNNING WATER
EVERY MODERN COMFORT

*An Ancient and Historic House
on the Great North Road*

Telephone: Telegrams:
Stevenage 42   "Cromwell Hotel"
                                                 Stevenage

Resident Proprietors:
MR. and MRS. RUPERT H. FRENCH

35 Advertisement for the *Cromwell Hotel*, c.1935.

As the 20th century advanced, the better-off began to acquire motor cars, inspired by the example of butcher Harry O'Clee, the first man in Stevenage to own a car. Charabancs were introduced as the modern version of coach travel and the Stevenage inns began to wake up again. The former *Cromwell Lodge*, owned at the beginning of the century by the Corbould-Ellis family, was converted into an hotel in the 1930s and earned itself an enviable reputation as one of the best along the Great North Road. Its gardens, designed and planted by Clarence Elliott of the Six Hills Nursery, became one of the main attractions of the High Street, with its delicate planting of alpine species set among grey stone and small conifers. At night it was further enhanced by lights twinkling through the trees, reflected in the clear waters of the ornamental pond. Not surprisingly, the *Cromwell* had its eminent guests, including the distinguished conductor, Sir Henry Wood, after whom the BBC Promenade Concerts are named.

Both the First and Second World Wars brought troops on foot, in tanks and in army lorries. In 1936 the Jarrow marchers, on their way to petition parliament, were welcomed and refreshed as they passed through the town. Finally, both the Great North Road and the Great Northern Railway brought the first New Town to Stevenage and, recognising the impact that motor vehicles were already making on the town—by the 1950s it was becoming positively dangerous to cross the High Street—the planners incorporated a sweeping new road to bypass Stevenage, to be designated A1 (M). When the bypass was opened in 1962, Stevenage had become so congested that it was welcomed with relief. Yet, there is a certain nostalgia for the days when the directions for a drive to Edinburgh were: 'Turn right into the High Street and continue for 375 miles along the Great North Road'.

Chapter 4

The Church

The history of every town and village in England includes a great deal about the religious life of the place. In the case of Stevenage, its history is doubly dependent on the Church because, since at least 1062, apart from one very short break, its lord of the manor has been a religious foundation. This influenced the atmosphere and ethos of the town as well as its economic and social development and its relationship with London.

Every piece of land in England is owned by some person or institution. At the time of the Norman Conquest not only the land, but the people and buildings on it, were owned nominally by the king. He could reward his supporters by granting them the right to hold certain lands, possibly including whole towns or villages. The lord of the manor did not necessarily live in the manor house, which was often occupied by a steward on his behalf. This arrangement was necessary in Stevenage, where the lord of the manor was the Abbot of Westminster Abbey. Towns and villages in the ownership of one individual were often overshadowed by his presence in the manor house, as he and his family exerted a powerful influence over the lives of his tenants. This has never happened in Stevenage. The old Bury (equivalent to a manor house) next to St Nicholas' church, is built on homely and unpretentious lines. The influential Lyttons of Knebworth acquired increasing amounts of land in Stevenage from the middle ages, including the manors of Cannix and Homeleys, but were never lords of the manor of Stevenage.

Because Stevenage was held by Westminster Abbey, there was continual traffic between Stevenage and London. In the middle ages tenants did not pay rent in money but in service. This might consist of a set number of days ploughing the lord's fields, helping with the harvest, repairing roads or transporting corn and other produce to Westminster.

The Westminster monks almost certainly had a small religious house in Stevenage, probably at or near the present site of Woodfield in Rectory Lane. They would supply a priest to take services at St Nicholas' Church and to farm the glebe land. The Saxons who gave Stevenage its name of *Stigenace* may have built

36 Ancient steps to the belfry in the tower of St Nicholas' Church.

35

a wooden church in their hilltop village, which would have been administered by travelling priests. During the 12th century a strong flint and stone tower was built, the oldest existing part of St Nicholas' Church today. The tower was not only part of a religious building, it also provided shelter for the villagers if danger threatened from bands of marauders or during time of war.

The earliest surviving record of a rector of Stevenage is that of Nicholas FitzSimon, who was inducted in 1213. He was appointed by the Abbot of Westminster, who held the advowson (that is, the right to appoint a priest to the living). The 13th-century rectors paid a pension of 50s. to Westminster Abbey and they in turn were supported partly by tithes from their parishioners. A tithe was one tenth of a person's income or produce and it was usually paid in kind; for example, in bushels of wheat which were stored in great tithe barns. No such

barn remains in Stevenage now, having been destroyed in the 19th century.

In the middle ages, the Church was of central importance to people's lives. Their year was a combination of natural, farming and religious seasons. At a time when few people could read and many led the harsh lives of subsistence farmers, the church services provided colour, light and music. Wall paintings taught them the Bible stories they were unable to read for themselves; carvings, stained-glass windows and painted rood screens, together with the chanting of the choir and dramatic presentations from the rood loft, all reinforced the Christian teaching that permeated their lives. They attended church for Sunday mass, baptisms, weddings, funerals, saints' days and days of penance. Those who could afford it made provision in their wills for candles to be lit at the altar and requiem masses to be said in their memory.

37 St Nicholas' Church, *c.*1945.

38 A farm cart passing St Nicholas' Church and cottages. The church spire can be seen above the trees.

It is interesting that, even though the Stevenage centre of population had moved away from St Nicholas' Church and Bury by the late 13th century, extensive rebuilding and enlargement was carried out to the existing church building at this period. The present chancel was added in about 1330, the nave aisles were widened and the font was installed. At about the same time, a spire of traditional Hertfordshire design was erected above the tower. During the same era the height of the roof may have been raised and subsequently lowered again in a future century. Evidence for this is the presence today of a door leading from the tower into space; presumably at one time it was enclosed by a higher nave roof. The beautiful misericord seats in the choirstalls were carved during the 15th century.

One possible reason for the continuing care and enlargement of St Nicholas' Church, even

though it was now remote from the main village, may have been the fact that there were many distant hamlets and farmsteads throughout the parish which would not have been much better served if a new church had been built in the High Street. In any case, most of the land between St Nicholas' Church and the town belonged to the Church, including the meads and fields through which ran the footpath which connected the village with its church. Some wealthy landowners in outlying places had their own chapels. For example, in 1308 John de Broxbourne was granted a licence to built his own oratory, or chapel, for private prayer at his manor of Cannix to the south west of Stevenage, later known as Broomin Green.

By the 15th century Stevenage, like many other towns, including Hitchin, had a guild or brotherhood of devout men who met together to pray and do charitable work. Some

39-40 Misericord seats in the choir of St Nicholas' Church. The carving on the left is of a woman with a scold's bridle in her mouth, to stop her talking. The carving below is of an angel.

guilds also ran schools, but there is no definite proof that this happened at Stevenage. Dedicated to the Holy Trinity, the Guild had its own Brotherhood House, with six acres of land, on the Bury Mead. The Guild was much respected in the town and men frequently left it money in their wills. John Anderson, haberdasher, who died in 1544, made several bequests to the church, including 6d. for a wax taper, 8d. for a rood loft light and 12d. to the Brotherhood of Stevenage.

Stephen Hellard, who became rector in 1472, is remembered as one of the first recorded benefactors of Stevenage. Shortly before his death in 1506 he himself had been bequeathed a newly-built dwelling and in his will he gave instructions for it to be used as almshouses for the needy poor, together with the income from six acres of land. The almshouses were to be called 'All Christian Soul House' and the residents were asked to pray daily for Stephen Hellard's soul. The almshouses, although no longer known by the name their founder willed, are still standing in Church Lane and fulfilling their original function.

A memorial brass to Stephen Hellard is to be seen in St Nicholas' Church today, in the same incomplete state as when it was put in place in the 16th century. Much has been made of the fact that the brass was probably designed and inscribed in Hellard's lifetime, with a space for the date of death which has never been added. The usual assumption is that he was in some way a vain or pompous man, anxious to ensure that he had a suitable memorial, but there could be many other reasons for the incomplete inscription.

During the reign of King Henry VIII, England's monastic foundations were dissolved and their lands and possessions handed over to the Crown. The lesser monasteries were dealt with first, from 1536, followed in 1538 by the greater. In 1539, in accordance with the royal decree, the Abbot of Westminster gave up his lands, including Stevenage. The king then created a new Bishopric of Westminster, which took over the manor of Stevenage. It is possible that, although the repercussions of the dissolution have echoed down the centuries, at the time the change did not make too great an impact on the daily lives of most Stevenage people.

In 1537, a new abbot had been appointed to the great abbey at St Albans. His name was Richard Boreman de Stevenage, often known as Richard Stevenage. He was appointed at an inauspicious time and in 1539 he had little choice but to sign away the abbey to the king. However, he was paid off with a substantial pension and survived the next 10 troubled years to re-establish St Albans School in 1551, in the reign of the Catholic Queen Mary.

In 1550 Stevenage changed hands yet again when the new Bishop of London was appointed lord of the manor. From that date, apart from a short break from 1649-60, it remained the property of successive Bishops of London until 1868, when the Ecclesiastical Commissioners took over. They remain lords of the manor to this day, with much reduced

powers, confined to such matters as use of common land. However, also in 1550 the advowson (the right to appoint the rector) was separated from the ownership of the manor. For the next 350 years the advowson was bought and sold, like any commercial commodity, by private individuals. The right to appoint all Church of England clergy in Stevenage is now in the hands of the Bishop of St Albans.

The rector of Stevenage during the confusing and dangerous times of the English Reformation and counter-Reformation was Thomas Alleyne. He was appointed in 1541, as Henry VIII's dissolution of the monasteries was beginning, and he died in 1558, a few months before the Catholic Queen Mary. He was almost certainly Protestant in his sympathies, as he is known to have attended the public burning of the martyr Bilney in Norwich in 1531. However, Thomas Alleyne managed to keep his position, despite the persecutions inflicted on the country by Catholics and Protestants alternately.

Alleyne is now mainly remembered in Stevenage as the founder of Alleyne's Grammar School but, more than that, there

41 Extract from the will of John Anderson, haberdasher, of Stevenage who died in 1544.

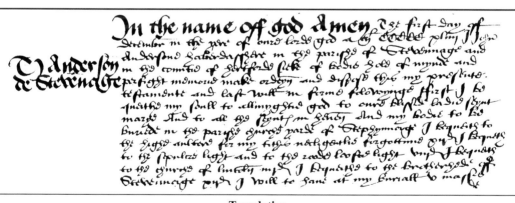

Translation

In the name of God, amen. The first day of December in the year of our Lord God 1544, I John Anderson, haberdasher in the Parish of Stevenage and in the county of Hertford, sick in body, whole of mind and perfect memory, make, ordain and dispose this my present testament and last will, in form following. First I bequeath my soul to Almighty God, to our Blessed Lady Saint Mary and to all the saints in heaven and my body to be buried in the parish church yard of Stevenage. I bequeath to the high altar of my tithes negligently forgotten 12d. I bequeath to the sepulchre light and to the rood loft light 8d, I bequeath to the Church of Lincoln 4d. I bequeath to the Brotherhood of Stevenage 12d. I will to have at my burial 5 masses ...

42 Almshouses in Church Lane, bequeathed by Rector Stephen Hellard in 1506.

is evidence that he was a good and trusted friend to his parishioners in his lifetime. Unlike many rectors, he actually lived in the town. In the days when many people were still unable to read or write, it was a blessing to have an educated man to help in time of trouble. Many Stevenage wills refer to Rector Alleyne with gratitude and affection, often appointing him executor. John Anderson, who died in 1544, directed in his will:

> I will that all my lands, tenements with all and singular their appurtenances ... be sold by Master Alleyne now parson of Stevenage unto whom I have declared my secret mind ... And that mine executors ... do nothing without the consent of the said Master Alleyne.

It is probable that Rector Alleyne lived in the house now called Woodfield in Rectory Lane, or in another building on the same site. It was not until the 18th century that the rectors of Stevenage moved into the new Rectory, now called The Priory, a little further up the lane on the opposite side.

At sometime during the English Civil War between 1640 and 1660, St Nicholas' Church suffered the loss of stained-glass windows, the whitewashing of murals and the destruction of other ornaments. In common with much of Hertfordshire and the eastern counties, Stevenage was probably sympathetic to the Parliamentarians, but how local people reacted

to the desecration caused by loutish behaviour on the part of some of the Roundhead followers is not known. Nor are the names of the rectors for this period, if any, recorded.

By the end of the 17th century, religious affairs in Stevenage had largely settled into their accustomed pattern, but there were those who could not accept the teachings of the Church of England. In 1676, 10 of them admitted publicly to being Dissenters, but it was not until 1689 that the Toleration Act made it legal for them to practise their faith. On 14 June 1698, Thomas Packet, Henry Farrow and George Heath signed a certificate stating that they would meet for religious worship at the house of Thomas Packet.

Another Rector who made an outstanding contribution to Stevenage was Nicholas Cholwell, who was appointed in 1738. He took a lively interest in the activities of his parish and historians owe him a special debt for the *Memorandum Book*, which he began in 1764. It opened with the words:

> A memorandum Book in which [are] to be registered from time to time, as they occur, an account of all matters and events relating to the Parish and Rectory of Stevenage, to be transferred to all future rectors for their use and information and by them to be continued.

In this *Memorandum Book*, Cholwell kept meticulous records of Stevenage land, owners and occupants, with detailed accounts of the tithes and rents paid by parishioners. His successors did continue the book for almost 100 years and there was an attempt to revive it in the early 20th century, when newspaper cuttings were stuck to blank pages. Another of Cholwell's legacies to the town was his planting, in 1756, of lime and horse-chestnut trees along the middle section of the path leading from the High Street to St Nicholas' Church, thus creating the nucleus of the Avenue which has given pleasure to Stevenage people for over 200 years. He also planted similar trees along the footpath between the Bury Mead and the Rectory.

It used to be the custom for the parish priest to lead his congregation on an annual perambulation known as 'beating the bounds'. Its purpose was to make sure that young people knew the extent of their parish in the event of a future boundary dispute. A perambulation took place on 28 and 29 August 1728, when Rector Thomas Stamper led his people in procession around the parish, starting at Whitney wood, 'at the corner of a close called Dunghill Land'. A measuring wheel was used to check the distance, which proved to be eight poles short of 14¼ miles. Perambulations were also held in 1758 and 1777, then discontinued until the next century.

Meanwhile, nonconformity was spreading in the Stevenage district. An academy was set up in 1799 at Little Wymondley to train young men for the nonconformist ministry. It remained there until 1850, subsequently moving to London to become part of New College, Hampstead. When the Wymondley Academy opened a chapel at Stevenage on 29 September 1814, there was widespread support from nonconformists in other towns. The inaugural service was led by Mr. Browne of Buntingford and Mr. Geard of Hitchin. Mr. Chaplin of Bishops Stortford preached.

The Methodists had been much encouraged by a visit from their founder himself. John Wesley preached in Stevenage in November 1790, at 87 years of age. In 1799 a Methodist Chapel was opened in the High Street, in the building now occupied by the Old Town Library. It was registered in 1799 by Robert Noddings, Joseph Cooper and James Bardel. From then on, the Methodist church in Stevenage continued to grow, although it had its difficult times until, in 1876, a substantial new chapel was opened at the south end of the High Street, next to the *Coach and Horses* inn, on the site where formerly open-air services had been held.

A Baptist chapel was opened in Albert Street in 1857. One of its early preachers was Henry Fox, father of the twins born the same year, whom he named Albert Ebenezer and Ebenezer Albert after the Ebenezer Chapel in Albert Street. The Bunyan Baptist Chapel, still flourishing in Basil's Road today, was built later, as was the Roman Catholic Church of the Transfiguration in Grove Road. In the first half of the 20th century the Salvation Army was also active in the town, holding open-air services accompanied by a band. Its first headquarters was the wooden hut on the corner of Baker Street and Church Lane.

In 1834 George Becher Blomfield became rector. His brother was the Bishop of London and lord of the manor of Stevenage. He arrived at a time when Stevenage was a prosperous coaching town, with a steadily increasing population. Church services were held every Sunday at 11 a.m. and 3 p.m. in the church and at 6.30 p.m. in the recently opened National Schools. The ancient church of St Nicholas, besides being now too small to accommodate all his congregation, was also in a bad state of repair. The rector energetically took all this in hand. He enlarged the church by building an extension from the south aisle, which was opened in 1841. In recent years it has been converted to a parish room.

As the rector dealt with the leaking roof, the draughts and the discomfort of the church, he made some drastic alterations which were not all well received. As was common in many churches, St Nicholas' had a musicians' gallery at the west end, supported by two pillars. The Rector had the gallery removed and the pillars taken down, to enable repairs to the structure of the building. Neither the gallery nor the pillars were replaced and the latter were later

43 Holy Trinity Church choir, *c.*1930, *above*.

44 Basil's Road Bunyan Baptist Church outing, *c.*1930, *left*.

45 Stevenage Band of Hope, 20 July 1910, *below*.

46 Harry Hawker, *above*, was for many years churchwarden at Holy Trinity. Here he can be seen at St Nicholas' Church lychgate, *c.*1965.

47 The south end of Stevenage High Street, *right*, before the one-way system was introduced. Holy Trinity Church clock, given by 19th-century parishioners in memory of Canon Blomfield, shows the damage done by pigeons. In the background is the *Coach and Horses* and, just visible, the Methodist Church. The photograph was taken *c.*1975.

48 Stevenage Rectory, *below*, seen from the back, painted by G. Oldfield, 1804. This building, subsequently enlarged, ceased from being used as the Rectory in 1919 and is now known as the Priory.

allowed to be taken to the Grange, where they still support the front portico.

Meanwhile, it was obvious that the greatest area of growth was in the south end of the town, where the building of Albert Street and the houses along the London Road were intended to cater for the increasing population. It was also decided that a new church should be built, as a chapel-of-ease, or annexe, to St Nicholas'. The rector prevailed upon his brother, the Bishop of London, to give a piece of land for this purpose. He did so, selecting a site which, while convenient for the High Street, was of no commercial value and consisted largely of the pond between the *Coach and Horses* and the Straw Plait Market, with the Southend Farm and Pound Farm beyond. Before the site could be used, the pond had to be filled in with cartloads of soil brought by the farmers. Over 100 years later Holy Trinity churchwardens were still coping with Bishop Blomfield's legacy in the form of regular flooding of the cellar.

The new church, named Holy Trinity, perhaps in acknowledgement of the medieval guild, was designed by another of the rector's relatives, his nephew, the architect A.W. Blomfield who was then embarking on his career. The builders were the Stevenage firm of Bates and Warren. The new church, opened in 1862, was almost immediately too small and an extension was built in 1881, under the guidance of Rector William Jowitt, who took office in 1874. Foremost amongst the wealthy families who helped support it were the Barclays of Whitney Wood. When Dr. Andrew Whyte Barclay died in 1884 his widow undertook to built a new chancel and stained-glass window in memory of her husband. This was completed in the following year.

Rector William Jowitt was the last of the old-style rectors, who had money of his own to help to finance his church and who threw himself whole-heartedly into every sporting, civic and social activity of the town. He was the natural representative of Stevenage at such county events as the Marquess of Salisbury's garden party, attended by Queen Victoria at Hatfield House in 1887.

The late 19th century saw the development of the temperance movement, whose aim was to combat the evils of drink. Its leaders included many clergy, who were only too well aware of the suffering caused by the misuse of alcohol. The Stevenage branch of this movement was slow in forming, partly because the rector was less than enthusiastic about it. The *Hertfordshire Express* of 7 April 1883 reported: 'We understand that it is at last decided to establish a branch of the C. of E. Temperance Society in this parish. Sermons will be preached on Sunday next ... setting forth ... the reasons why it is desirable to established a branch in Stevenage'.

The Rector's sermon must have been something of a disappointment to temperance supporters. He began by saying that he was only preaching on the subject because he had promised to do so, but 'I would much rather have been excused'. He quoted some statistics, such as the fact that Stevenage had one public house for every 25 adult males, but added that 'wine makes glad the heart of man' and is only harmful in excess. However, a Stevenage branch of the Church of England Temperance Society was formed and became quite strong, giving regular entertainments at the Town Hall and supporting a band of its own.

The 20th century brought many changes. A new rectory was built in 1919, during the incumbency of Canon Molony, who succeeded Rector Jowitt. It was sited a few yards higher up Rectory Lane from the former rectory, which became known as the Priory. During the development of the New Town, a church was built in each neighbourbood and, after initial experiments with team ministries, each became a parish church with its own vicar. St Nicholas' was stripped of its ancient rôle as the parish church of Stevenage, and its priest no longer holds the title of rector. As the reorganisation continued, it was deemed expedient to sell the 'new' rectory, which was demolished to make way for the houses in Chestnut Walk.

Chapter 5

Education

Weekday mornings in the late 20th century see clusters of children, rushing, skipping or dawdling along the Avenue to school, just as children have done for at least 700 years. The Bury Mead property of the Church has been a site for education since the middle ages and possibly before. The earliest surviving written record of a school in Stevenage is dated 1312; although its location is not given, it is probable that it was situated on or near the Bury Mead. The record, from the annual report of the bailiff or steward of Stevenage to the Abbot of Westminster, details the cost of keeping William le Rous at school in Stevenage:

For the board of William, son of Sir Richard le Rous, being in The Schools at Stevenage from the feast of St Mark the Evangelist to St Michael's day

22 weeks 3 days, 18s. 8d. (that is 10d. a week)

For three yards of blue cloth bought for a tunic and a hood for the use of the same, 3s. 9d.

For making the same with a pair of sleeves of the robe of the same, 8d.

For two caps bought for the use of the same, 3s. 8d.

For shirts, 2s. 0d.

For one pair of Stockings & two pairs of shoes, 20d.

49 Alleyne's Schoolhouse as it was in 1800 from a watercolour sketch by G. Oldfield.

The school attended by William Le Rous could have been associated with St Nicholas Church as a kind of choir school and it is possible that it continued into the 15th and 16th centuries. The Guild of the Holy Trinity, which is known to have existed at least as far back as the mid-15th century, may well have had some involvement with, or even total responsibility for, the school or its successors.

Thus, when Rector Thomas Alleyne died in 1558, having provided in his will for the foundation of a free grammar school at Stevenage (as well as one each at Stone and Uttoxeter), it is almost certain that a school already existed there and his bequest was intended to refound and upgrade it, rather than create an entirely new institution. It is even possible that Mark Dauné, the man named in Alleyne's will to be headmaster of the new establishment, already had this position in the existing school.

After a generous start, in which he expressly ordered that all children within two or three miles of Stevenage who had reached the required level of education should be admitted into his school, Alleyne went on to lay down strict rules of behaviour. Between Michaelmas and Lady Day (30 September to 25 March) scholars were to be in school before 7 a.m. and between Lady Day and Michaelmas they were to arrive by 6 a.m. They were allowed a lunch break from 11 a.m. until 1 p.m. and could go home at 5 p.m. Prayers and psalms were to be recited three times daily in Latin, and all conversation was to be in Latin. Scholars were not to swear, follow dishonest practices or keep evil company, but were to 'behave themselves gently to all kinds of persons of every degree' and were to love and reverence their schoolmaster.

Pupils who did not observe their founder's rules were to be caned and, to ensure an adequate supply, every pupil enrolling at the school was required to pay two pence towards the cost of canes and also towards the upkeep of a poor scholar, whose job it was to keep the school clean.

50 Alleyne's School in 1931.

51 The pavilion at Alleyne's School was in a field across from the Avenue. The pavilion was built by the carpentry class, shown in the photograph, and completed 3 July 1896.

52 A classroom at Alleyne's School, c.1916. In the middle row, extreme left, is Howard White; on the extreme right is Cyril Richardson.

Shortly after Alleyne's death another school was founded, or refounded in Stevenage. In 1561 Edward Wiltsheir, who had recently acquired land formerly belonging to the Guild or Brotherhood of the Holy Trinity, left it to Sir John Boteler and other Stevenage men who were raising money by public subscription for the purpose of setting up a school in the town. This school was to be for 'Pettits' or smaller children, with the intention of teaching them English. It could be likened to an elementary school, whereas Alleyne's school was for pupils who had proper command of the English language and were qualified to learn Latin, which was the main purpose of the school. Despite the obvious difficulties of teaching

children within a wide range of age and ability, the Pettits' School and Alleyne's School agreed to share premises newly built with Edward Wiltsheir's legacy in the 1560's. This is the building still in use today and known as the Old Schoolroom.

Unlike Alleyne's School, whose governors were the Master, Fellows and Scholars of Trinity College, Cambridge, the Pettits' School was under local control, having been founded with money raised by local people, and as such it continued to attract support. Edmund Nodes left the Bury Mead for the use of the school in his will of 1596, and his grandson John Nodes gave it additional land 35 years later. In 1601 Robert Gyne gave three roods of arable land

53 Old maltings in the High Street was mistakenly identified by a plaque as the original Alleyne's School building.

in Church Field and Edmund Woodward gave £12 yearly to the master of the school for the education of children in 'good literature'.

Meanwhile the Grammar School followed the directives of its founder and educated its scholars in the classics, to a high enough standard to prepare them for university. In 1639 William, son of William Clarke of Chesfield, was admitted to St John's, College Cambridge, after seven years at Alleyne's Grammar School. An equally scholarly pupil was Henry Chauncy, who studied at the school from 1641-46 and was later to become the county's first historian with the publication of his *Historical Antiquities of Hertfordshire* in 1700.

There was inevitably some friction between the two schools, the main problem being the reluctance of the Grammar School masters to teach the Pettits. In 1632 the Commissioners of Charitable Uses had confirmed that the school building should be used 'to teach scholars called Pettits to read English, write, cast accounts and learn the accidence'. The Commissioners made it clear that the master of the Grammar School had a right to use the building for his own scholars, but was expected to teach the Pettits also. In 1672, the Court of Chancery decreed that the master must teach the Pettits as well as the Grammar School scholars, and that the Pettits should be

admitted to the Grammar School, if they reached the requisite standard of education. But the decree was not obeyed and in the following year the Master of Alleyne's School was dismissed for refusing to teach the Pettits.

During the next 100 years, Alleyne's Grammar School declined so far from the standards prescribed by its founder that by the early 19th century it was little more than an elementary school of which it was said 'only by a great stretch of terms that classics can be said to form a part of the curriculum of this school'. However improvements were made and by the end of the century the school was recognised as Alleyne's Grammar School and administered by a board of governors including representatives from Trinity College, Hertfordshire County Council and Stevenage Urban District Council. Day boys and boarders between the ages of eight and seventeen were admitted, thus merging the two foundations into one school.

With growth it became imperative to provide more accommodation, since the school still met in the original 1562 Pettits' School. In 1905 under the headmastership of R.G. McKinlay, new classrooms, cloakrooms and master's room were added and the school continued to expand. Following the 1944 Education Act it took its place in the state education system as a grammar school. In 1969, in common with many other Hertfordshire schools, it became a comprehensive and its name reverted to Alleyne's School. Twenty years later an even more startling change occurred when the former Stevenage Girls Grammar School merged with Alleyne's to become the Thomas Alleyne School.

During the mid-19th century a rather unusual occurrence had resulted in two competing schools operating almost next door to each other. The Rev. John Osborne Seager, who was also a curate in the town, had been appointed headmaster of Alleyne's School in 1836, at a time when it was at its lowest ebb and complaints from parents were numerous. In 1847 he bought the old *Swan Inn*, now sadly in decline, and renamed it the Grange School. He left Alleyne's and took most of his fee-paying pupils with him. During the next 50 years he built up the Grange School, so that it acquired a considerable reputation; pupils came from all over England, including three future bishops, the future Earl of Chichester and Lord Teignmouth.

Since he was also licensed as curate of the parish of Stevenage, John Osborne Seager led

a full life as recorded in his obituary notice of 1889: 'indeed he seems to have been connected with almost every public work in the district for the last half century'. He retired from teaching in 1883 and bought Springfield, a substantial house facing the Grange, where he lived in active retirement. After his death a memorial service was held, when,

> ... in a larger assemblage than we have ever before seen on such an occasion ... neighbours from near & far, Churchmen and Dissenters, rich and poor, stood side by side and testified ... to their appreciation of the noble and upright character of one who had so long lived among them fulfilling well the words of his family motto *Fidelis Amicis*— Faithful to Friends.

On his father's retirement the Rev. John Lingen Seager took over the school. As headmaster he admitted young Edward Morgan Forster, probably at the suggestion of the rector's wife. The boy was made desperately unhappy there by the bullying and uncouth behaviour of his fellow pupils, although he spoke warmly of Mr. Seager's ability as a teacher. Some 30 years later Jack Franklin, who lived only yards from the Grange, was

54 Alleyn's Road, named in memory of Rector Thomas Alleyne, using one of the variant spellings of his name. The correct pronunciation, whatever the spelling, is 'Alan's'.

55 Girls' class at St Nicholas' School, 1904-5.

56 A girls' keep-fit class in the town hall, *c.*1916, photographed by Mr. Howard. The girls were from St Nicholas' School and Hitchin Girls' Grammar School and the classes were led by Miss Roden, a mistress at St Nicholas' School. *Back row, left to right*: Winnie Field, ?, Nellie Barker, Winnie Merrington, Centerina Cooper, ?, - Merrington, Doris Day, ?, ?, ?, - Hawksworth.
  Middle row, left to right: Nellie Wallace, Hilda Clewlow, - Bowyer, - Bowyer, Miss Roden, Nellie Newberry, Litchfield, Agnes Allen, ?.
  Front row, left to right: ?, Doris Kings, Edith Upton, Elizabeth Newberry, Miriam French.

also a boarder there. He too has unhappy memories of the school where, under the head-mastership of Mr. Nicholls, boys were flogged for the least fault. As he walked away on his last day, it gave him great satisfaction to fling his school cap down in the gutter.

During and after the Second World War, the Grange gave shelter to children from the home at Briar Patch, Letchworth, whose premises had been burnt down. After this the Grange continued its educational rôle, providing overflow classroom accommodation for St Nicholas' and Alleyne's schools and for a short time acting as the first home of the new Stevenage Girls' Grammar School. Today it is used as the Stevenage Divisional Education Office and The Stevenage Registry Office.

When Thomas Alleyne wrote that 'all manner of children' might be admitted to his school he probably assumed boys only, as did the Seagers at the Grange. Although it is fairly certain that the early Pettits' School admitted girls, little provision was made locally for their education. Wealthier families could engage governesses to teach their daughters, but girls from the poorer classes were probably taught only practical skills such as straw-plait making, although there may have been a dame school which attempted to give them the rudiments of education.

It was not until the 1830s that plans were made to provide elementary education for all the town's children, boys and girls alike. Under the leadership of the rector, the Rev. R.G. Baker, money was raised by local residents to build a school and master's house. Land at Bury Mead was leased to the rector and the churchwardens by the lord of the manor, the Bishop of London and all the funds for the project were raised by subscription, the chief contributor being an anonymous 'Friend of Stevenage' who gave £100. Other sub-scribers included; the Master and Fellows of Trinity College, Cambridge; the Bishop of London; the rector; the Misses Kinaston, keepers of the Bury Mead; Mr. W. Parkin of Chesfield Park and Mr. T. Franklin of North Road. The total cost was £709 3s. 11d., which included £2. 17s. 0d. paid to the well-digger for digging a 19ft. well at 3s. 0d. per foot, and £4 for a school bell. The master's house, the only part of the building still standing today, cost £191 7s. 6d.

Notices advertising the new school were displayed in the town, requesting parents who wished to enrol a child to attend at the School

Rooms between 10 a.m. and 1 p.m. on the appropriate day, when information would be given to them about rules of the school, age of admission and the weekly payment expected for each child. Those living on Main Street (High Street) were to attend on Thursday, 19 December 1833; those in Back Lane, Letchmore Green or near the church on Friday 20 December; and those living in the remoter hamlets of Fishers Green, Symonds Green, Pin Green or 'any other place' on Saturday 21 December.

The response was good and the rector was pleased to note that when the school opened on Wednesday, 1 January 1834,

> although not a single parent had been visited to send a child, nor a child asked to attend, and although a weekly payment was expected from everyone ... 116 boys and 91 girls attended, having been previously admitted ...

57 St Nicholas' School in 1958.

The buildings were also used for other purposes, including vestry meetings, church services and the Stevenage Magistrates' Court.

In 1851 improvements were made, and extensions added to provide a separate room for the infants. At the same time, ownership of the site, replacing the previous lease, was conveyed to the rector and churchwardens. Twenty years later, following the 1870 Education Act, a public meeting of the inhabitants, presided over by the rector, Canon G. Blomfield, voted to increase the accommodation and, after some bureaucratic delays, this was carried out. There were increased numbers of children on the registers—in 1882, there were 196 in the girls' department—but many children were very irregular attenders. Successive Inspectors' reports despaired of the poor attendance which eroded the excellent work being done by the teachers. In times of financial hardship it was tempting for parents to allow children to work in one of several brickfields in the town, or to stay at home making straw-plait.

Until 1910 there were three schools, or departments, in the Bury Mead buildings; Boys, Girls and Infants. By 1910 the numbers had become so great that a new school, built by Hertfordshire County Council for boys only, opened in Letchmore Road. For many years it was under the headmastership of Mr. Roach.

The school celebrated its centenary in July 1934. The programme included:

> Festive Procession of 400 scholars, starting from Holy Trinity Church and proceeding via the High Street to the Grammar School sports field. The procession will be headed by the Dr. Barnardo's Boys Band and by a group of children in the costume of 1834.

In the evening there were maypole dances on the lawn of Whitney Wood, home of the Barclay family, followed by excerpts from *A Midsummer Night's Dream.*

At the turn of the century, the official name of the school was 'Stevenage Church of England School'. Later it became known as 'St Nicholas' School' and in 1950, when Miss F. Lawrence was headmistress, its present uniform was designed, with a badge showing the bishop's mitre and three bags of gold from the legend of St Nicholas. In 1966, the school moved to a new site in Six Hills Way.

During the 19th and early 20th centuries there were various private schools in Stevenage. Mrs. Beaver and her daughters ran schools from a succession of premises, including no. 35 High Street, a house in Stanmore Road and another at Six Hills. Westover School, on the corner of Julian's Road and Hitchin Road, was run by Miss Ruth Culley. Her sister, Mabel, who taught art, had studied at the Slade School and was an accomplished water-colourist. Her *Stevenage Picture Book*, published during the 1940s, is a brief record of the town as it was in her lifetime.

The 1944 Education Act had promised 'secondary education for all' and raised the school leaving age to fifteen. In order to accommodate children over eleven who were not going on to a grammar school, the first secondary modern school in Stevenage was built in Walkern Road, with playing fields backing onto the Avenue. It was named the Barclay School, after Mary Barclay, the last member of the Barclay family of Whitney Wood, who died in 1946.

Its modern architecture was different from all other schools in Stevenage and it won high praise from Dr. Nikolaus Pevsner. In his *Buildings of England* volume on Hertfordshire he described it as 'free and felicitous' and was specially interested in the main staircase 'carried up on a concrete spine'. A statue by Henry Moore, entitled *Family*, placed at the entrance door was rather too modern for some people when it first appeared and green paint was poured over it. Now it is recognised as one of the treasures of Stevenage.

Chapter 6

Law and Order

It is unfortunately true, in the words of Shakespeare, that, 'The evil that men do lives after them'. Records of offenders brought to justice at manorial and assize courts ensure that the names of wrong-doers, or those accused of wrong-doing, have survived the centuries.

In the middle ages the settlement of local disputes and the upholding of law and order was largely done in the manorial court, which in Stevenage was held in the Bury. Five courts a year were held by the Abbot of Westminster at Stevenage in the 13th and early 14th centuries. Profits from fines levied at the courts in the year 1271-72 amounted to 43s. 3d. and in 1320-21 to 69s. 2d. The number of courts and the dates on which they were held varied over the years, but they usually coincided with a religious feast or saint's day, such as St Andrew's Day (30 November), St Matthew (21

58 Stanmore Road Health Centre was built on the site of the former Stevenage police station and court-house. The weather-cock is from the original building. The photograph was taken in 1987.

55

September) or the Annunciation of the Blessed Virgin Mary (25 March).

The types of offence dealt with at these courts seem comparatively minor today, but they were a great source of annoyance to neighbours and ultimately, if left unchecked, harmful to the community as a whole. Offences such as failing to keep hedges trimmed or ditches scoured, and of course theft, were the most common. In 1377, for example, John Hamond was fined for carrying away corn from the lord's field.

Punishments were crude, including the pillory and stocks, in which offenders were held fast while righteous villagers pelted them with abuse, rotten eggs and rubbish. A ducking or cucking stool was frequently used to punish scolds (nagging or abusive women) by ducking them in a pond. Stevenage had all three corrective devices, sometimes at the request of the villagers themselves, rather than by any imposition of their masters. In 1409, it was pointed out to the Abbot of Westminster that he was 'bound' to have a pillory and cucking stool in the village, and that the cost of them should not be charged to the inhabitants. The Abbot ordered his bailiff to supply them. In 1542 the stocks were repaired and a new pillory and cucking stool were provided.

For a time the King himself had a prison in Stevenage, and it is recorded that in 1310 the release was ordered of Andrew Baron who, on being accused of larceny, had fled for sanctuary to St Nicholas' Church, whence he was removed by 'certain malefactors' to the prison.

The court records of the 16th and 17th centuries emphasise how closely almost everyone was tied to the land. Robert Heath was ordered to 'lay off' the lord's waste ground which he had taken into his close (in effect he had stolen a piece of rough land by fencing it) before 24 December, under penalty of £1 a pole. John Williamson was ordered to fill in his ditch next to his ground in the Hoppit before the feast of St Michael, under penalty of 10s.

In 1682 it was ordered that no person should drive any cattle into the common fields to feed there until 'they be ridd' (gleaned); penalty 13s. 4d. No cattle were to be fed on the baulks (headlands) in the cornfield and no one was to cut grass on the baulks, penalty 13s. 4d. Anyone having a ditch or watercourse leading from Bury Mead or Temditch Wood to the further end of Bedwell Mead, or from Broming Lane End to Ded Boy Lane End was ordered to scour it immediately, under penalty of 2s. 6d. per pole. Baulks and grips (roadside baulks) were to be made up before the next May Day, penalty 4d. No one should put sheep in the cornfields until nine days after 'they be ridd'.

Apart from these local laws, there were also the laws of the realm to be obeyed, and those who broke them and committed more serious crimes were tried at the Assize Court, the nearest being at Hertford. Theft, or larceny, was the most persistent offence, and punishments were severe. At the Hertford Assizes on 4 March 1573, Richard Robynson, glover and Richard Whyte, shoemaker of Stevenage, were found guilty of burgling the house of Richard Hunt at Stevenage and stealing a silver spoon worth 4s., five pairs of linen sheets worth 10s. and two veils worth 2s. They were sentenced to hang.

Some names crop up several times in the Assize records, until an individual's run of luck ends. Richard Tydye, a Stevenage labourer, was accused at the Assizes on 5 March 1585 of stealing a sheep worth 2s. from John Clark and another sheep worth 8s. from Thomas Thurlebye. He was found not guilty; the next year he was back in court, accused of stealing seven sheep and a lamb worth 40s. from Thomas Clarke at Ayot St Lawrence and 13 sheep and two lambs worth £4 from Richard Bygge at Kimpton. He was found guilty, but avoided punishment. In 1591 he was accused of stealing sheep and lambs from John Lylly, John Fuller, William Curtice and William Broke at Letchworth. This time he confessed and was sentenced to hang.

Belief in witchcraft was still prevalent in Elizabethan times. At the March 1587 Assizes Agnes Morris, spinster of Stevenage was accused of bewitching Richard Jenkinson five years earlier on 1 July 1582, so that 'he languished until May 1 1583 and then died'.

Minutes of the Stevenage Vestry meetings dating from 1575 give a clear picture of local affairs through three centuries. Vestry meetings were originally committees dealing with church matters, but their scope had gradually broadened until they became responsible for most aspects of life within English towns and villages. The rector was *ex officio* chairman of the Stevenage Vestry and the churchwardens were also bound to attend. All householders of the town had the right to come to meetings and had to be encouraged to play their part in local affairs by the promise of food and ale. In this respect Stevenage differed from many other towns, notably Hitchin, where a few wealthy men took it upon themselves to exclude the majority of inhabitants and to keep the vestry 'select' by co-option instead of election.

Vestry meetings usually took place in a public house, such as the *Swan* or the *White Lion* in the High Street and the *Royal Oak* in Walkern Road, except at Easter, when it was customary to meet in the parish church to elect the churchwardens. The responsibilities of the vestry were numerous. Apart from administration of the Poor Laws, which took up a great deal of time and money, the health and security of the town were its concern. For example, recurrent epidemics of plague made it essential to provide somewhere away from the town where victims could be isolated. To meet this need the Vestry had the Pest Houses built in 1765, high up on the edge of the town, near the mill and not far from the church, just off the road to Weston. The site is now called Mount Pleasant.

Fighting crime was another concern of the vestry. From the middle ages onwards two unpaid constables were elected annually, and were officially appointed by the Justices of the Peace, who themselves were appointed by the Crown. This worked well at first but, as the population increased, the limitations of a voluntary system became obvious. In the 18th and 19th centuries propertied people began to

59 The door of the first Stevenage police station in North Road.

form associations and pay ex-soldiers and other suitable men to patrol their towns and protect their homes. A Stevenage Residents' Association was formed in 1807, each member contributing money and promising to use all his energies to catch offenders. Rewards were offered to informants, and the association was quite successful in preventing crime. However it became obvious that this arrangement, too, was inadequate and in 1841 the Hertfordshire Quarter Session voted to levy a rate to establish a paid police force. There was violent opposition to this in some quarters, particularly from such landowners as the Marquess of Salisbury, Samuel Heathcote of Shephall, and 68 'persons of substance' in Hitchin, none of whom wished to contribute towards protecting other people's property.

Stevenage police station was at first a cottage in North Road, and later in Orchard Road next to the Town Hall. Much of the time and energy of the 19th-century police was taken up by poachers, particularly the notorious Fox twins, Albert Ebenezer and Ebenezer Albert, who took care never to go poaching together and were so alike that they could use the excuse of mistaken identity. Born in 1857 in Symonds Green, the twins were named after the Baptist Chapel or 'Ebenezer' in Albert Street, of which their father Henry Fox was a devout supporter. Their mother was a straw-plait maker.

With such a respectable background it is not clear why the Fox twins took to a life of crime. Some people consider that they actually preferred poaching to earning an honest living,

60 Albert Ebenezer and Ebenezer Albert Fox.

others that they were 'wrong 'uns' from the start, and yet others that they had become embittered by treatment received in their youth from their 'betters' and genuinely believed that no one man had the right to own land and its wildlife. Whatever the reason the Fox twins' poaching careers made local and national news. They were said to be among the first to assist in the evaluation of a new method of identifying criminals through fingerprints, discovered by Sir Edward Henry. In spite of the twins' way of life, many local landowners had a grudging affection for them, and helped them out from time to time.

Both twins ended their days in Chalkdell House, Hitchin, formerly the workhouse. Ebenezer died in 1926 and Albert in 1936. The *Hertfordshire Express* reported that the only two people present at Albert's funeral were Lady Fellowes and the Hitchin historian Reginald Hine. They left a wreath of irises with the inscription:

> Gone to earth old friend
> And lost to mortal view
> Good luck to you where'er you wend
> Fresh woods and pastures new.

The more serious crime of murder occurred occasionally over the centuries. In 1613 Anne Corye, wife of miller Henry Corye, was brought to trial at Hertford Assizes, accused of poisoning her former husband John Tattersall. Unfortunately there is no record of the verdict and it remains a mystery whether Anne was a murderer. The site of the old mill, which is today overshadowed by the Lister Hospital and the much enlarged *Mill*, a Beef-eater restaurant and motel, retains the name Corey's Mill. It is also the place where the footpath which was once part of the ancient Roman road from Verulamium via Wheathampstead emerges into the Hitchin Road. Over the centuries Roman soldiers, pilgrims, merchants, King Charles I in disguise, all have passed through here to and from Baldock. The mill was well sited at a busy crossroads, and no doubt Henry Corye, the miller, was a very prosperous man. However, it would be wrong at such a distance in time and with no evidence to attempt to

61 Corey's Mill, *c.*1918. The inn was known as the *Harrow* in the 18th century, but was changed to the *White Horse* in 1769. In recent years it has been renamed the *Mill*.

judge whether or not his wife Anne was guilty of murder.

No such scruples worried the local newspapers in the 19th century. The murder of Police Constable John Starkins, whose body was discovered in a pond near Norton Green in 1857, was the subject of widespread comment. When Jeremiah Carpenter of Six Hills was arrested for the murder, the *Hertford Mercury* had no doubt that he was guilty. On Saturday 7 November 1857 its report stated categorically, 'The evidence against the man is so conclusive that there cannot be the slightest doubt as to his being the party or one of the parties guilty of this atrocious death'. Since the trial had not yet taken place and very little evidence, for or against

Carpenter, had been made public, the newspaper was guilty of unfounded assertions.

In fact, there was more than the slightest doubt that Carpenter had committed the murder, although there was also strong evidence against him. He was apparently long suspected of poaching and of the petty theft of corn from his employer, Mr. Horne of Norton Green Farm. More damning, he had been heard to threaten violence against the local police for questioning him. On the other hand, there was some doubt as to whether he could have been at the scene of the murder at the time it took place and there was much conflicting evidence.

From the day that the body of poor Constable Starkins was taken to the *Chequers*

Inn in London Road, the crime was the main topic of conversation among local people and continually reported with much speculation in the press. An inquest was held by Mr. Times, attended by Captain Robertson, Chief Constable of the county, and 'a posse of police officers'. A reward of £50 was offered for the apprehension of the murderer. On Wednesday 24 November 1857, Carpenter was taken to the Church School (i.e. St Nicholas School) on the Bury Mead, to face the local bench of magistrates, the Reverends E. Prodgers, J. Harding, S.H. Knapp and Mr. Morris Pryor. They committed him for trial at Hertford Assizes and he was 'conveyed to Hertford Gaol in a closed carriage. A large crowd of people assembled in front of the school house to see him enter the vehicle.'

The trial itself was eventful and it was clear that some of the court officials had not carried out their duties properly. For example, the young daughter of one of the prison warders travelled in the gaol van with the prisoners, who were allowed, in contravention of the regulations, to talk to each other. During the hearing a PC Quint gave evidence that he had heard Carpenter admit his guilt. He was about to be cross examined when,

> The witness here fell down in a fainting fit. His coat and collar were immediately loosened but as he did not presently recover, the learned judge suggested that he should be removed into a cool room.

Inevitably, Quint's dramatic collapse was taken by some to indicate that he had committed perjury and was overcome by remorse.

The prosecution made much of the fact that there were traces of blood on Carpenter's knife, but the defence pointed out that there was 'not a labourer's knife in the kingdom which did not have blood on it.' At that time it was impossible to distinguish between human and animal blood; had forensic science been more advanced, the evidence one way or another might have been conclusive. As it was, the jury made an unusual statement, through their foreman, Mr. Ballard, of Watford: 'We all think there is great ground of suspicion, but not direct evidence enough to warrant us in finding the prisoner guilty. We therefore return a verdict of "Not Guilty".' Upon which the leader writer of the *Hertfordshire Mercury* for 13 March 1858 argued that the verdict was a strong argument against capital punishment, concluding 'the woodstealer and the pickpocket are shut up in prison while Cain goes at large, shriven by juries who believe him guilty'.

Chapter 7

Victorian Expansion

When Queen Victoria came to the throne in 1837, Stevenage was a prosperous small town. The 1841 census recorded that the population was 1,724 and there were 366 dwelling houses. The town consisted largely of the High Street, Back Lane (now Church Lane), Letchmore Green and the roads leading to Walkern, Weston, Hitchin and Baldock, together with the scattered farms and hamlets of the parish.

The larger houses had their own wells or pumps but many of the villagers had to rely on pond water. There were no street lights and few pavements, even in the High Street. The coaching era was at its peak and Stevenage inn-keepers, brewers and blacksmiths were flourishing; but the town was still predominantly an agricultural one, with most people earning their living from the land.

62 Letchmore Road and Holy Trinity Church, *c.*1905. From left to right; Mr. Shelford, 'Lord' George Shelford, Cissie Shelford, later Mrs. Boorman.

A source of annoyance throughout the country at this time was the continuing practice of paying tithes, a tax equivalent to one-tenth of the harvest of the land, which had to be paid annually to the titheholder, who was often, but not always, the parish priest. In Stevenage the only titheholder was the rector. Originally tithes had been paid in kind, for example in bushels of wheat or other produce. Over the centuries, individual agreements were made between those who paid and those who received the tithes, that they could be paid in money, although there was no standard rate. The Tithe Commutation Act of 1836 went some way towards redressing the unfairness of the situation by ensuring that all tithes were converted to rent charges, which were regulated annually according to the price of corn.

Fortunately for local historians, the Stevenage Vestry decided in 1834 to order a survey of land in the parish, in connection with the apportionment of tithes. The resulting map, drawn up by John Richardson of Cambridge, has proved an invaluable record of land ownership and use in Stevenage in the early 19th century. Of the 4,300 acres of the parish, 70 per cent were arable land, 20 per cent pasture, eight per cent woodland and two per cent dwellings. Some of the field names that existed then have been adopted as road names, for example Aldock, Haycroft, Longcroft and Whitesmead Roads. Others are now obliterated, or only alive in the memories of those old enough to remember Stevenage before it became a New Town; names such as Pancake Corner, Swallow Close, Rabbit Dell, Stockings, Further Stockings and the intriguing Great Blacknose and Little Blacknose. Post House Meadow, between London Road and Ditchmoor Common, is believed to have been the field where horses were grazed while resting between shifts pulling the mail coaches. Postmead, the house built there in the 19th century, was pulled down 100 years later during the building of Fairlands Way.

63 Fairlands Farm in 1804, from a sketch by G. Oldfield. The last herd of cattle in Stevenage was sold here in 1957.

64 Fred Archer in Posting House Mead, London Road, 13 September 1889. Ditchmore Common can be seen in the background.

In the 1830s many of the High Street's buildings were either inns or farms. At the south end of the town, was the *Coach and Horses*, formerly the *New Inn*, where the landlord was one who proudly advertised the horses ready in his stables for changing teams when the stage coaches rolled into town. On the other side of the road were the *Chequers* and the *Marquess of Lorne*, which had started life as a small brewhouse but enlarged its trade during the coaching era. Almost next door to the *Coach and Horses* was the Workhouse, then Pound Farm and Southend Farm, with their fields beyond. Together this group of buildings encircled the open space where the straw-plait market and the town cage or lockup faced a large pond.

It was at the south end that the town's population was increasing most rapidly, with many of the poorer people crowded into small cottages in Back Lane and Letchmore Green. Labourers and craftsmen were among those living here, employed on the farms, or in one of the several brickfields in Stevenage, such as that in what is now Brickkiln Road, or at Six Hills. A large percentage of the working class was in domestic service of some kind, including employment at the town's many inns.

The increase in population was the reason for the development, in mid-century, of a completely new street named after the Prince Consort, Albert Street. It was intended to be a shopping street for Stevenage and to provide up-to-date houses for rent, to replace some of the insanitary old cottages. By today's standards the houses, mostly terraced and fronting directly on to the street, had drawbacks. However they had sizeable back gardens and were much appreciated by their

65 Stevenage railway station was opened in 1850. The photograph shows the waiting rooms in about 1920.

66 Julian's Road in the early 1900s.

67 Holy Trinity Church, *below*, was built in 1861 on the site of one pond, and facing another. To the right is the *Coach and Horses*. The thatched barns in the background belonged to Southend Farm.

STEVENAGE, HERTFORDSHIRE.

Particulars and Conditions of Sale of

FOUR COTTAGES,

(TWO OF WHICH ARE COPYHOLD,)

Situate near the Back Lane, in the Town of Stevenage, in the several occupations of Mrs. TAMPLIN, SMITH ALDRIDGE, CHARLES GRAY, and BOTTOMS; together with an

ENCLOSURE OF OLD PASTURE LAND,

Having a Frontage to Church Lane, near to Road leading from Stevenage to Walkern, containing about ONE ACRE, in the occupation of Mr. J. CHALKLEY;

By direction of the Trustees under the Will of the late Mr. William Belgrove;

ALSO A

BRICK-BUILT & TILED COTTAGE,

In Middle Row, in the occupation of WILLIAM WADE, at a rental of £5 4s. 0d. per annum;

By direction of the Trustee under the Will of the late Miss Ann Belgrove;

TO BE SOLD BY AUCTION, BY

MR. GEORGE JACKSON,

AT THE WHITE LION INN, STEVENAGE,

On MONDAY, September 18th, 1865, at 3 for 4 o'clock.

PARTICULARS.

LOT 1 will comprise **2 Timber-built and Tiled Freehold Cottages** with joint use of Yard, situate in Pratt's Yard, near the Back Lane, in the occupation of Mrs. TAMPLIN and SMITH ALDRIDGE, each containing 2 Bed-Rooms, Sitting-Room, and Wash-house, at rentals amounting to about £8 per annum, Landlord paying Rates and Taxes.
Bounded by Property belonging to Mr. H. Piggott and Mr. Pratt.

LOT 2 will comprise **2 Timber-and-Thatched Cottages** with Wood-Barn and Piece of Garden Ground to each, situate in Church Lane, near to road leading from Stevenage to Walkern, in the occupation of CHARLES GRAY and BOTTOMS, at rentals amounting to £7 16s. per annum, Landlord paying Rates and Taxes.
Bounded by Property belonging to M. Pryor, Esq., and Mr. H. Piggott. *The above is Copyhold of the Manor of Stevenage.*

LOT 3 will comprise a **valuable Enclosure of Old Pasture Land**, containing about 1 Acre, well situate near the road leading from Stevenage to Walkern, having a Frontage to Church Lane, and is a suitable site for building Cottages upon, now let to Mr. J. CHALKLEY, at a rental of £3 per annum.
Copyhold of the Manor of Stevenage, and sold subject to the present Footpath across the same; the Timber to be taken at such sum as shall be stated at the time of Sale. Bounded by Property belonging to M. Pryor, Esq., Mr. Venables, and Mr. J. Chalkley.

LOT 4 will comprise a **Brick-Built and Tiled Cottage**, in Middle Row, in the occupation of WILLIAM WADE, at a rental of £5 4s. 0d. per annum.

N.B.—The Dwelling House with Grocer's Shop, lately occupied by Mrs. Belgrove, together with the Dwelling House adjoining, as previously advertised, will not be Sold.

May be Viewed previous to the Sale by permission of the Tenants, and Particulars had at the Inns in the Neighbourhood; of Messrs. Jackson and Son, Auctioneers and Estate Agents, Hertford and Ware; of R. H. Peacock, Esq., Solicitor, 3, South Square, Gray's Inn, London; and of Mr. George Jackson, Auctioneer and Appraiser, Hitchin and Baldock, Herts.

68   An 1865 sale notice for cottages in Back Lane, Church Lane and Middle Row.

occupants who enjoyed the neighbourliness and the convenience and interest of living in a street where shops and houses intermingled. There were drapers', tobacconists', butchers', grocers' and bakers' shops and at least one general store. Two non-conformist chapels were built here, including the Ebenezer Chapel where Baptist Henry Fox preached. Two public houses, the *Prince of Wales* and the *White Horse*, completed the amenities.

In 1847 the navvies building the Great Northern Railway arrived in Stevenage. There were large numbers of them and they were not always welcomed by everyone. A Navvy Mission Room was opened in Albert Street, to provide an alternative to the many public houses in the town, where the men could rest and relax. In 1850 Stevenage railway station was opened at the top of Julian's Farm Road.

Once the station was in operation several new roads were built in the vicinity. New-comers, many from London, were attracted to live in the pleasant country town of Stevenage, now so conveniently situated on the Great Northern Railway. In rapid succession Julian's Road, Essex Road (part of which was originally named Percy Avenue) and Railway Street were built. The latter, in spite of housing Stevenage's new town hall and po-lice station, quickly acquired a reputation as a street of ill-repute and was largely demolished and rebuilt by John Bailey Denton of Orchard Court, who renamed it Orchard Road. In recent years it has been cut in half by Lytton Way and the High Street end given its third name of James' Way, after the jeweller whose shop once stood on the corner.

John Bailey Denton, who contributed a great deal to the town apart from his official duties, was appointed Assistant Enclosure Commissioner for Stevenage following the General Enclosure Act of 1845. Before this Act, most arable land in the town was in large unfenced fields, each of which was divided into strips, or plots. This ancient system was in many ways inefficient, as each plot had a different owner; conversely, one individual might have several plots in a number of fields, scattered throughout the parish. For example,

John Horn had 28 acres of land in 28 different plots. To complicate matters still further, owners often let their plots to others to farm. But the system also had advantages, including giving villagers the right to graze their animals on common land.

John Bailey Denton's first duty was to carry out a survey of the land in Stevenage on behalf of the Enclosure Commissioner, Sir Edward Lytton of Knebworth. Lytton was also the largest landowner in the parish. From the middle ages there are records of the Lyttons steadily acquiring property in Stevenage, much of it in the south and west of the parish, where it adjoins Knebworth. When the survey was complete, the enclosure awards were made; that is to say, farmers were offered combined acreages of land which they were required to fence. Robert Trow-Smith points out that,

> The rationalized allotments devised by the enclosure commissioners spelt the doom of the small farmer. Faced with the costs of fencing them, he sold out to his larger neigh-bours ... The result was that by the beginning of the 20th century the land of Stevenage was in the hands of the farmer of wide acres.

The changes in farming and the appearance of the countryside was echoed by changes in the town. The arrival of the railway brought about the end of the coaching era and thus the decline of those trades that were dependent upon it, such as innkeeping. The great cattle market disappeared and the annual fair became a pleasure fair only, no longer an important business occasion. The railway divided the town, since crossing it was a dangerous procedure; places such as Norton Green and Broomin Green became even more cut off than previously.

Communication between Stevenage and London was now easier and quicker and new ideas began to take root in the town. Farm labourers' wages in Hertfordshire in the 1860s averaged 11s. or 12s. per week, less than those of railwaymen and most other workmen and far below wages in big towns, or in London itself. Although the incomes of many families were supplemented by the straw-plait industry,

69-70 Two views of the Bowling Green. Note the cyclists, *below*, on the Hitchin Road who are on their way home from the ESA.

71 Charles Tompson (bearded) and his wife, Sarah Maria, pose together with their son, Alfred, and daughter, Frances, with their market cart at Norton Green, *c.*1890.

72 Charles and Sarah Maria Tompson took over the tenancy of Norton Green Farm in 1843.

73 Sarah Maria Tompson (centre) outside Norton Green Farm, *c*.1900.

74 Alfred Tompson seen here on horseback at Norton Green, *c*.1905.

Hertfordshire labourers were beginning to feel that discontent with their condition which had previously led to riots in surrounding counties. They did not resort to similar action themselves, but many supported the founding of the National Agricultural Labourers' Union (NALU) in 1872. The following year several branches were set up in Hertfordshire, including one at Stevenage, to the alarm of some of the farmers and clergy.

In July 1873, Mr. Culpin of the Stevenage Branch of the NALU chaired a mass meeting at Butts Close, Hitchin, which was addressed by the founder himself, Joseph Arch. In the next few years, farm workers' wages did increase somewhat, but almost immediately Hertfordshire farming began to suffer even more than other counties from the effects of cheap imports of food from the United States and the British Empire. Bad harvests caused a further decline and, to make matters worse, income from straw plaiting disappeared, as Britain began to import cheap straw hats from China and Japan. Many small farms,

including that of Mr. Howard at Rooks Nest, failed altogether and the farmers moved out, selling their property cheaply to larger land-owners. The Howard family had farmed at Rooks Nest for over three hundred years, when, in 1882, they sold up to their larger neighbour, Colonel Wilkinson of Chesfield Park.

While some farmers were leaving, others survived. In 1843, Charles and Maria Tompson took over the tenancy of Norton Green Farm, part of the Knebworth Estate at the extreme south-west boundary of Stevenage. Their son, Alfred Tompson and his wife, kept going during the difficult times by taking in paying guests. They were fortunate in that the Stevenage Golf Club, which at that time consisted mainly of a large field, was immediately opposite their farmhouse and a steady stream of visitors was attracted to stay here.

The employment situation in Stevenage improved when the Educational Supply Association (ESA) opened its premises in Stevenage, opposite the station, in 1883. For

75 Stevenage Golf Club at the turn of the century, when the course consisted of a field behind Norton Green pond.

76 The south end of the High Street, 1920, showing horses drinking at a water trough and children playing beside the pond. The Co-operative store on the right was in premises attached to the *Coach and Horses*.

77 'New Town' Post Office on the corner of Lymington Road and Fishers Green Road, *c.*1902.

78 ESA 'A' shop workers, 1950/52.

79 The ESA factory, *above*, at Holmsdale Terrace, Fishers Green Road, was built in 1883.

80 Silk's ironmonger's shop, *left*, on the corner of Green Street and the High Street, *c*.1885.

81 A membership certificate of the Stevenage Provident Society, 1888.

the next 100 years it was a major employer in the town. Four times a day, with clockwork precision, the High Street would be filled briefly with bicycles as ESA workers cycled to the factory, home to lunch, back for the afternoon shift and home again at dusk.

The ESA also built homes in the town for its workers. Basil's Road was one of the first, named after the managing director's son. The development of a number of roads off Fishers Green Road, including Huntingdon, Southsea, Lymington, Bournemouth and Jubilee Roads, became known as 'New Town.' Here, as well as the corner shop run by the Scarborough family, there was the New Town Post Office, grocery and baker's shop combined, on the corner of Lymington Road and Fishers Green Road. It was run by Alice Tompson and her husband, a horse dealer with a yard and stables behind the shop.

Collecting times for the New Town post box were 7.30 and 9.30 a.m., 3 p.m. and 7.50 p.m. The first Post Office in Stevenage had been at no. 61-63, High Street, the black and white building later known as Chamber's Library and currently Forbuoys Newsagent's. In 1887 a new, purpose-built post office was opened at no. 52 High Street—next door to what is now Elmes' Arcade—before it moved again into new premises almost opposite, at no. 13. Its latest move, in 1994, was across the High Street to be incorporated into the Waitrose shop at no. 74.

In 1890, as well as the main Post Office and the New Town Post Office, there was a pillar box in the Market Place (at the top of Middle Row), a wall box in Orchard Road and another at the South End of the town. In the 20th century one of the whitewashed cottages in London Road became the

82 O'Clee's butcher's shop Christmas display in 1900. These premises are now occupied by Lloyd's Bank.

Southend Post Office, much loved by residents until its demise in the 1960s.

Gas was provided by the Stevenage Gas Company Ltd., formed in 1855 and occupying the former workhouse in Letchmore Road. Since the Poor Law of 1835 Stevenage had become part of the Hitchin Union of Parishes. This meant that the aged and destitute of the town were now sent to the Union workhouse at Hitchin, not a happy ending for those who had spent their lives in Stevenage. Some limited insurance against poverty was provided by the Stevenage Provident Society, formed in 1830, which had 402 members by 1890. Its principal services were to pay out cash to members during sickness and to defray burial expenses.

The affairs of the town were now in the hands of an elected Local Board. Members in 1890 were; Rev. William Jowitt, M.A., Rector (Chairman); David Austin of Letchmore Green; Edwin Bays of London Road; Samuel Chittenden of Bowering, London Road; Charles Culpin, boot and shoe dealer, Registrar of Marriages and Overseer of the Poor; Thomas Ellis, grocer, High Street; Lewis Fresson, chemist, High Street; Herbert Matthews, veterinary surgeon, Berkeley House, London Road; Joseph Moulden, butcher, High Street; Frank Moules, dairyman, High Street, Seymour Nash, High Street; John Smith, B.A., Upper Bury (i.e. Old Bury).

In 1871, the Stevenage Police Station had moved from its former home in North Road, opposite St Nicholas' School, into new premises adjacent to the new Town Hall. The Stevenage magistrates' court was also transferred to the Town Hall and Petty Sessions were held there on the second and last Thursday in every month at 12 noon. Chairman of the bench in 1890 was the forceful personality of Unwin Unwin-Heathcote, of Shephalbury. His fellow magistrates were; the Rev. John Cotton Browne of Walkern Hall; John Bailey Denton of Orchard Court; Rear Admiral Thomas Butler Fellowes, C.B., of Woodfield, Rectory Lane; George Hudson, M.A., of Frogmore Hall; Humphrey Jones, C.B.; Marlborough Pryor, M.A. of Weston Manor; Charles Poyntz Stewart, M.A. of Chesfield Lodge. William Onslow Times was clerk to the magistrates.

83 The new post office in the early 20th century.

84 Males' shop on the corner of Walkern Road and the High Street, *c.*1911. 'Twinkle' Males is in the doorway.

Telephone STEVENAGE 184

WURR & Co.

(K. G. WURR)

HOUSE AND ESTATE AGENTS
INSURANCE BROKERS

LIST OF AVAILABLE HOUSES AND
ILLUSTRATED GUIDE SENT GRATIS
AND POST FREE ON APPLICATION
TO

18 HIGH STREET
STEVENAGE - - - HERTS

85 Advertisement for Wurr and Co., estate
agents, *c.*1935. In the 19th century William Wurr
was organist and choirmaster at St Nicholas'
Church.

The Town Hall was also used for more
light-hearted activities, including the amateur
dramatic entertainments so beloved of the
Victorians. Considerable sums of money were
raised for charity, as well as providing a great
deal of enjoyment. The untiring efforts of
people such as William Wurr, the parish
church organist, whose annual 'Coal
Concerts' provided money for the poor to
buy fuel for the winter, helped to alleviate
the lot of the elderly, unemployed or sick
villagers for whom life would otherwise have
been very cold and miserable.

Stevenage knew how to celebrate when the
occasion arose. The Golden Jubilee of Queen
Victoria in 1887 provided just such an
opportunity. E.V. Methold, local historian,
described the occasion:

> After a service and children's sports, a
> dinner was given to everyone in the parish
> over the age of 15. Over 1,100 people sat
> down to the meal, assembling first on the
> Bowling Green, whence they walked in
> companies of 46 to the tables, which were
> placed down the High Street and covered
> by tarpaulins lent for the occasion by the
> Great Northern Railway. The Rector and
> the oldest woman in the parish led the way.
> The gentry of the town carved. The provi-
> sions were; 2,000 lbs beef; pickles, 1 gallon
> for each table of 46 persons; new potatoes,
> 1 bushel to each table; plum pudding, 1 lb
> per person, and bread. Also 1 pint beer or
> ginger beer per person. Everything passed
> off well and I did not hear a bad word or
> see any drunkennness the whole day.

Chapter 8

Country Town

At the time of the 1901 census, the population of Stevenage had increased to 3,957, over three times what it had been in 1801, after a century of steady growth. For comparison, during the same period Hitchin's population had also increased by about three times, Graveley's had almost doubled, but that of Shephall, after reaching a peak of 265 persons in 1841, had declined to 194 in 1901.

Although more people were now employed in shops, domestic service and, since the arrival of the ESA, in industry, Stevenage remained predominantly a country town, with most people dependant on the land to a greater or lesser extent. The Board of Agriculture statistics for 1905 showed that, of the town's 4,545 acres, 3,200½ were arable land, 916 permanent grazing or pasture and 325½ acres were woods. The remaining 103 acres were dwelling houses and other buildings, equalling approximately two per cent of the total area. This proportion was unchanged since the 1841 census.

Many observers have commented on the lack of industry in Stevenage at this time despite its good road and rail links with London. The accepted reason for this is that, since the middle ages, landowners have seen Hertfordshire, including Stevenage, as a rural retreat for sporting and farming uses. The editor of the *Victoria County History of Hertfordshire*, volume 1, published in 1902, reached the same conclusion:

There are few counties in England where game is more strictly preserved for shooting than in Hertfordshire. This county, though adjacent to the metropolis, has yet retained to a great extent its rural character; it is therefore, almost as a matter of course, looked upon as the natural sporting ground of those who are obliged to make London their home.

There is consequently a great demand for shooting all over the county, and at the present time it would be difficult to find a farm or a covert that is not preserved.

Stevenage people were used to this state of affairs, but they did not all accept it meekly. Poaching was a serious offence, punishable by transportation or imprisonment, but that did not stop it going on night after night in the woods around Stevenage. There was war between poachers and gamekeepers as each plotted to outmanoeuvre the other. The Fox twins happened to become famous but they were only two of the many poorer people for whom poaching was a way of life. Many a Stevenage pheasant was supplied by poachers to a ready market in London, or even locally, where some of the better-off were prepared to turn a blind eye from time to time.

As for the so-called vermin—stoats, weasels, rats, mice, voles and birds such as magpies, jays, owls and hawks—they were likely to end up on the keeper's gibbet. Anyone entering Whomerley Wood was faced with one of these grisly lines of dead bodies, strung up not so much as a warning, but to prove to the landowner that the keeper was doing his job. In the season, shooting parties would enjoy a day's sport, sometimes ending with a formal photograph of the gentry, their servants, dogs and a few local boys proudly showing off the day's 'bag' of pheasants, partridges and plover.

86 A shooting party in Whomerley (pronounced 'Humley') Wood, *c*.1900.

At this time, there was a developing interest in the scientific study of wildlife. The comparatively new art of photography was an invaluable aid and, although cameras were large and heavy, enthusiasts such as the great pioneer nature photographer, Richard Kearton, were producing magnificent photographs which stirred the interest of the nation. Stevenage was fortunate enough to persuade Richard Kearton to lecture at the Town Hall, as one of a series of Cambridge University Extension lectures being held there.

However even though some people were beginning to take to the camera rather than the gun, the accepted method of ornithology was still that of shooting rare or unusual birds and keeping a collection of their stuffed bodies. The *Victoria County History* notes that the first Hertfordshire record of the Arctic or Richardson's Skua was that of one shot near

Stevenage in 1881. Charles Poyntz Stewart was recorded as the owner of a stuffed Reeve (female Ruff) which had been shot at his Chesfield estate. It was also reported that, although Black-headed Gulls were frequent visitors, Herring Gulls were 'quite a rarity in Hertfordshire, very few specimens having been obtained; but in the autumn of 1898 Mr. M.R. Pryor continuously saw small parties of Herring Gulls ... flying over Weston Manor near Stevenage'.

Not only birds but butterflies and moths were assiduously collected locally. Recorders throughout Hertfordshire worked on a voluntary basis to build up county lists of species and their distribution. Mr. Matthews was the recorder for Stevenage, maintaining detailed notes, and occasionally claiming a rarity. 'Mr. Matthews of Stevenage is able to report the capture of *Thecla Betulae* (Brown

Hairstreak) which has been taken sparingly in Norton Green woods, but is not recorded for any other Hertfordshire locality.' On the other hand, he reported that the moth *Halias Prasinana*, which was generally distributed throughout the county, was 'not at all common in Stevenage and that he has seen only two or three specimens'.

Although very much a country town, Stevenage had good communications with London. Many of its residents travelled there daily by train to work, others went on business or pleasure. There were those who had never been to London even in the early 20th century but, generally speaking, the people of Stevenage were in touch with the wider world outside and not just with their own parochial affairs.

When Queen Victoria died in 1901 and was succeeded by her son Edward VII, the town went into mourning, followed by celebrations as the new king was crowned. Bunting and displays stretched along the High Street and private houses put out their own flags. Pound Farm was swathed in union jacks and royal symbols, as were many other buildings throughout the town. On the corner of Basil's Road and Letchmore Road, opposite the *Dun Cow* on Letchmore Green, a row of modern cottages was built named appropriately Coronation Cottages.

New buildings were all about at this time. In 1905 Alleyne's Grammar School was considerably enlarged, including the building of a new dormitory (there were then about fifty

87 Pound Farm decorated for the coronation of Edward VII in 1901.

88-9 Coronation Cottages, Letchmore Road, were built in 1901. Albert Olieff, above right, in his back garden at Coronation Cottages before they were demolished, *c.*1967. Victoria Close was built on the site.

90 The top section of the Avenue, planted in 1935 to mark the Silver Jubilee of King George V, veers to the left of the old Avenue.

boys boarding) above the covered playground with four arches visible from the High Street. The following year New Road, a long straight road parallel to the railway line, was built by the Great Northern Railway Company. It ran from Broomin Green through Fairview Farm to the back of the station, where it joined Fishers Green Road. Residents of New Road were not happy with this uninteresting name and later persuaded the authorities to change it to Fairview Road. Land between the new road and the railway was leased to the Urban District Council as allotments, an arrangement which worked very happily until 1993, when British Rail sold it for housing development.

The trees which had been planted in 1887 to extend the Avenue to the High Street were by now maturing and forming a delightfully shady walk to St Nicholas' Church or, on a hot day, providing respite from the sun. At night it could be just a little eerie. In 1910 The Hertfordshire antiquarian, Gerrish, who made a study of local mythology and witchcraft, wrote a letter to the East Hertfordshire Archaeological Society, in which he referred to the legend of a ghostly black dog seen near Six Hills and Whomerley Wood. His letter struck a chord with E.V. Methold, builder and historian of Stevenage. He wrote to Gerrish:

> Last night I read Mrs. Methold your letter about the Ghost of a black dog to be found at Stevenage. She tells me the following but begs that you will not publish it or if you should feel tempted, to do it in such a way that it could not be traced to her as having supplied it ... She declares that she has seen it and on one evening *very* late she in company with others saw an object or shadow which appeared to rise out of the ground in the middle of the Bury Mead and come towards the Avenue where they were walking ... they saw the form of a large black dog approach with its head bent towards the ground and its tail curled over its back, one of the party whistled it. As it came nearer they saw the large size it was. It took no notice, passed by them and disappeared, its size as you described nearly as big as a donkey. I need not add they were much frightened.

On another occasion a gamekeeper personally known to me, saw the same apparition, near a field gate which opens on to a bye road to the Avenue. As he walked toward this gate the apparition of a large dog rushed by him passing through the closed fieldgate just in front of him, though much too big to pass between the bars...This man, accustomed to being out in the lonely woods night after night became so nervous that he returned back to the house of his friends, being too nervous to return alone to his own home.

Also there are others in Stevenage who have seen the same, mostly near the Avenue ...

For goodness sake I hope if you publish this you will not scare all the new inhabitants from the town for the town will become deserted and there are enough houses as it is to let this year in the place. I have one to let rent £85 can you find me a tenant ...

With regards I remain Yours sincerely
E.V. Methold

(Original letter in Hertfordshire County Record Office.)

A few years later other spectres were haunting the country. Letters home from Stevenage men fighting in the First World War tended at first to be cheerful and optimistic; they preferred not to tell their families the horrible details of life in the trenches. But the dreadful events of 1915, when so many thousands of British troops were killed, could not be hidden. Several Stevenage men wrote describing how they were saved from almost certain death by the Angel of Mons.

At home, working parties and relief funds were set up, to supply comforts such as knitted garments for the troops and financial support for those families left without their wage-earners. Mrs. Grosvenor, the doctor's wife, was one of those responsible for sending parcels to the troops. These were gratefully received, one young officer writing brightly: 'The parcel has arrived from Mrs. Grosvenor and I have dished out the woollies to the men'. At the Grange a War Workers' Department was set up where volunteers could make bandages and dressings to be sent out for the use of the wounded on the battlefield. Lady Fellowes, the former Margaret Jowitt, daughter of the rector and now wife

91 Church Lane in 1964. The Tower House and its neighbour were built by the Stevenage historian E.V. Methold at the end of the 19th century.

of Admiral Fellowes of Woodfield, was treasurer of the Soldiers' and Sailors' Families Association, just one of her many local charitable works. Mr. T. Seager Berry, Mrs. Heathcote and Miss Bailey Denton were some of the other leading residents who helped to organise working parties for the war effort.

Stevenage, on the Great North Road and the Great Northern Railway, received many Allied troops. Large numbers of them were billeted in private houses, such as that of the Taylors in Alleyn's Road, who mostly took British 'Tommies', or their neighbours opposite, who put up New Zealanders and Australians. The large premises at No. 29 High Street, on the corner of Basil's Road, was used as a billet and the soldiers there quite often had concert parties, watched from the street by crowds of local residents. A little further along, at the *Old Castle Inn*, the publican, George Gray, also billeted Austalian and New Zealand troops and provided a canteen for them. Those soldiers

unlucky enough to be without billets sometimes slept in Middle Row, where Mrs. Halling, from the *Buckingham Palace* public house, often took pity on them and allowed them to sleep in the bar.

The First World War was also the first in which aeroplanes were employed. Stevenage suffered at least one air attack, when bombs were dropped on Bedwell Lane, destroying barns. Similar attacks were taking place all around London and in December 1915 the Home Office issued a Lighting Order for Hertfordshire, requiring buildings to be blacked out after dark, to prevent their light from guiding enemy aircraft. Rector Canon Molony, a man with a dry sense of humour and a witty pen, remarked upon the sudden famine of curtain rings in the town. No doubt he would have enjoyed the story told by the Taylor family of Alleyn's Road. They had a German clock on their mantelpiece which stopped with dramatic finality when the bombs fell in Bedwell Lane. The family also recall looking out of their window one dark night and seeing a Zeppelin drifting down from the sky in flames. It crashed near Cuffley.

People at home suffered hardship, as essential supplies became difficult to get. There were riots in Hitchin and other towns because of food shortages. Stevenage, perhaps more self-sufficient and more used to growing its own vegetables and keeping chickens in cottage gardens, avoided these. But few could avoid the anguish of waiting and worrying about husbands, sons, fathers and brothers away on the continent, often out of contact for weeks or months at a time. The true horrors of the war were gradually brought home, as shell-shocked and physically wounded soldiers passed through the town, some on their way to the V.A.D. (Voluntary Aid Detachment Nursing Service) Hospital at Bragbury End. This was later moved to Knebworth Golf Clubhouse.

There was anguish too for the Belgian refugees who had escaped from their own country and found shelter in Stevenage. One young woman, who arrived expecting her first child, did not know if her husband was alive or dead. Local people shared her anxiety and even more her joy when, by a strange coincidence, her baby was born on the day news arrived that her husband was safe.

92 ANZAC troops were billeted in Stevenage during the First World War. In this photograph they are seen in the field behind the *White Lion*. Note the wooden steps leading from the field path to Bridge Road, which remained in place until Ivel Road was built.

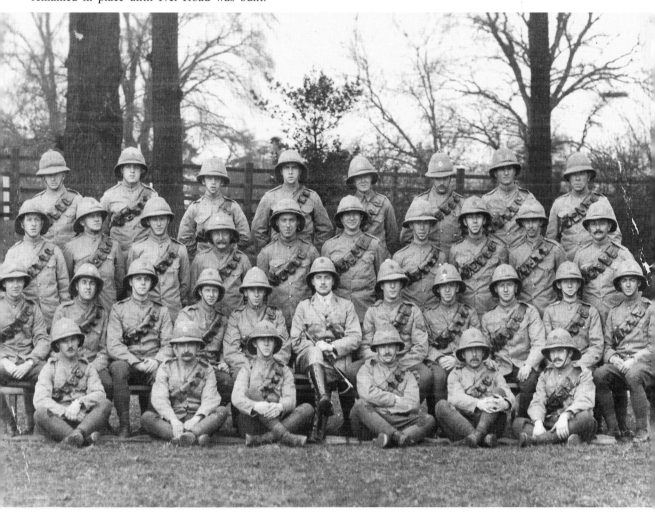

Long after the fighting ended, suffering and sorrow endured in many families. Hardly anyone was unaffected. In 1921 a memorial to the men of Stevenage who had lost their lives in the war was erected on the Bowling Green. Their names were also displayed in the churches. At Alleyne's Grammar School memorial gates were dedicated in 1920 in honour of former pupils who were among the dead, the money having been raised by subscription.

In the 1920's, traffic of various kinds increasingly passed through Stevenage. The railway loop line from Stevenage to Hertford and Moorgate was completed in 1923 and was to play a decisive rôle in the future of the town. On the road, motor vehicles were becoming commonplace and some of the old coaching inns, including the *White Lion*, began to offer garage services. It was motor traffic which prompted an irate letter from Mr. Corbould Ellis of Cromwell Lodge, High Street to the

93   The War Memorial on the Bowling Green was erected in 1921.

94 *Buckingham Palace* public house, *c.*1910.

Chief Constable of Hertfordshire, Colonel Alfred Law, on 29 June 1923:

> I beg leave to draw your attention to the lack of police supervision which we suffer from in this town. It appears that we have here an Inspector and 3 constables, possibly one of whom is a sergeant. One has to be at the station always, which leaves 3 for duty. These 3, however matters may be arranged, are except in cases of great emergency, eight hours on duty in every twenty-four ...
>
> It is a large district and the county rate is very heavy, and all one can ask is that we have sufficient police service so that the laws of safety may be obeyed and if not, action taken. The general complaint in this town is racing cars and the noise through motorcycles making a dreadful noise going through and about the town.

By this time the Stevenage police had new premises in Stanmore Road, built in 1916. Ironically, some of the labouring work was done by Albert and Ebenezer Fox, who posed cheerfully enough for photographs. The young Philip Ireton, born in Walkern Road, remembered the occasion with amusement all his life.

Cycling was popular during the early years of the 20th century, when parties of cyclists would arrive in Stevenage High Street after a day pedalling through the country lanes, eager for tea at Steer's restaurant. For some years, Steer's and the *Marquess of Lorne* opposite competed furiously in their attempts to win customers.

By the 1920s and '30s charabanc outings were becoming popular. Shopworkers, Sunday

95 The Boorman family reunited after the First World War.

96 The cycle shop at 115-17, High Street, photographed in 1912-13, when the Boorman family took over from Bookers.

Schools, the Club and Institute were among those arranging outings to the Derby, the seaside or other places of interest. Motor coaches were also providing services to Hitchin, the market town and centre of north Hertfordshire, to which all roads led. One essential service was that provided by Mr. Candler's North Star Coach, taking people to Hitchin Hospital for consultancy, treatment and operations. Those requiring prescriptions were expected to take their own bottle in which to bring back the medicine. Children who were to have minor operations such as the removal of tonsils were taken to hospital by coach in the morning, operated upon after being rendered unconscious by a chloroform mask, while their mothers and the coach waited to take them home in the afternoon. Primitive though this may sound in the 1990s, it had the advantage that children were separated from their mothers only for minutes, and were able to return to their familiar home surroundings immediately after the operation. By the 1940s the dreaded chloroform mask was still in use but the system had 'improved' to the extent that children were kept in hospital for three days, during which parents were not allowed to visit or make contact.

Before the National Health Act of 1948, those who could afford it paid for their medical care. Others could pay a small subscription into a locally organised scheme, which entitled them to treatment. In order to subsidise this scheme and to buy new equipment for Hitchin Hospital, fund raising events were arranged, the most memorable in Stevenage being 'Hospital Saturday'. Rather like today's Carnival, this involved shopkeepers, businesses and organisations processing through the town in their decorated, horse-drawn carts and traps, collecting money from bystanders. There was keen competition for the prizes awarded for the best outfits.

In the 1930s farming remained dominant in Stevenage, but there were increasing opportunities for other types of employment. As well as the ESA, there was the Stevenage Knitting Company, mainly employing women, which opened its premises in Sish Lane in 1927,

and the world famous Vincent HRD company based in the old maltings building next to Alleyne's Grammar School in the High Street. Between 1924 and 1927 the premises were occupied by Howard R. Davies, a well-known motorbicycle racing driver. His motorcycle design and manufacturing business had failed and was taken over by Philip Vincent. He named his company Vincent HRD (after H. R. Davies) and developed some of the most successful racing motorcycles in the world. He was later joined by George Brown, as mechanic and rider. The company finally closed in 1954, but for many years George Brown, followed by his son, ran a motorcycle shop opposite, on the other side of the bowling green. An annual George Brown Memorial Race is still run by the Vincent Owners' Club.

THROUGH

49

YEARS

FROM

1924

TO

1973

We have seen many changes in our 49 years at your service, but all that time we have led the way in safe and comfortable travel

NORTH STAR COACHES Ltd

Directors: A. W. Candler   P. M. Candler

STEVENAGE   LETCHMORE ROAD

PHONES: 54128 (office)

LUXURY COACHES ALL SIZES TO 53 SEATERS

DAY EXCURSIONS TO COASTAL

RESORTS

FROM EASTER TO 30th SEPTEMBER

97 Advertisement for Candler's North Star Coaches, 1973.

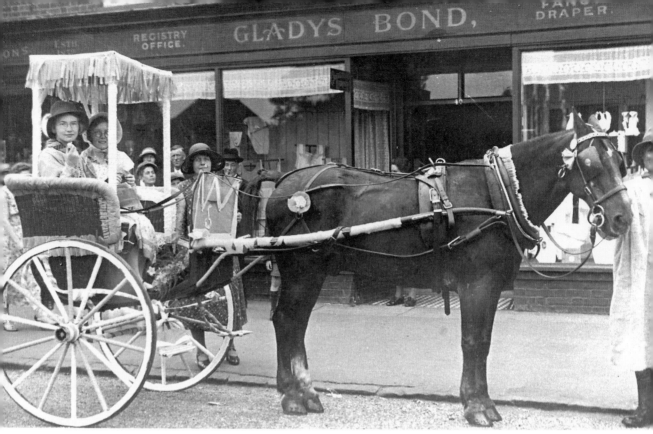

98 An entrant in the Stevenage Hospital Saturday parade.

99 Mrs. L. Wheatley (right) with a friend, taking her goats along Sish Lane to their pasture, which is now the site of Sish Close, *c.*1945.

100 An advertisement for Vincent HRD motorcycles, *c*.1945.

BRITAIN'S BEST
Motor Cycle
MADE IN STEVENAGE.

1935, 500 c.c. '' Comet '' Vincent H.R.D. - £86

Special features include Patented Spring Frame, Semi-o.h. Camshaft Engine, Four Brakes, Instantly Detachable Wheels, Patented Spring Pillion Seat, etc., etc.

The Largest Firm of Motor Cycle and Cycle Specialists in Hertfordshire

Our Retail Department carries large stocks of New and Second-hand Motor Cycles and Pedal Cycles. Spare Parts and Accessories.

Every kind of Repair promptly carried out.

Our Very Easy Hire Purchase Terms are famous throughout several Counties.

Agents for our products in most large cities overseas.

The Vincent "H.R.D." Co. Ltd.

Telegrams: Velocity Stevenage. | **Stevenage** | Telephone: Stevenage **206**

101 The Bowling Green in the mid-1940s.

102 & 103 The gardens at *Cromwell Hotel*, seen above and below left, in *c*.1965, were planted and designed by Clarence Elliott.

104 Clarence Elliott at his Six Hills Nursery, *c*.1945, *below right*.

Stevenage was a place of pilgrimage not only for motorcycle enthusiasts, but also for gardeners. From 1907 to 1954, Clarence Elliott operated his nationally famous alpine plant nursery at Six Hills. Even his catalogues were sought after as collectors' items because he had the perspicacity in 1920 to engage the services of a young artist named John Nash, then unknown. In 1976, Nash wrote of his first meeting and subsequent friendship with Elliott:

> This was the beginning of a long friendship with the Nurseryman, Plant Collector or, as he preferred it 'Gardener,' Clarence Elliott. I used to draw the plants he had collected on his expeditions to the Andes and the Falkland Islands and elsewhere, not excluding finds in English gardens which

he maintained were the best hunting ground. I was always at the ready to visit Stevenage if something special happened, such as the first flowering after several years of *Puya Alpestris* [a very prickly alpine plant] ... The first book I illustrated (in 1926) was the *Six Hills Nursery Catalogue*, a hundred copies of which my wife and I coloured by hand.

Many of the larger gardens in the town, including Cromwell Lodge, later the *Cromwell Hotel*, in the High Street, were designed and planted by Clarence Elliott.

Although motor traffic increased steadily throughout the first half of the 20th century, farmers, milkmen, and many tradesmen continued to use horse-drawn transport until well after the Second World War. The premises of Hutchinson's Bakery, at the top

105   Stevenage High Street, looking north, *c.*1935.

106   Steers' corner, at the south end of the High Street, *c.*1945.

107   The High Street, looking north, *c.*1950.

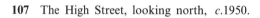

of Albert Street, included a small shop immediately adjacent to the yard where the cart horse was stabled. Customers would hear the clip-clop of his feet and smell the warm aroma of horse mingled with that of bread and cakes. Mr. Allen and Mr. Phipps, two of the town's milkmen, used horse-drawn floats, as did Mr. Allison, the saddler, at 82 High Street. Smartly turned out, Mr. Allison was the last to accede to the motor car and continued to drive along the High Street in his pony and trap until the 1970s.

Stevenage had blacksmiths' shops, on the Bowling Green, at the South End and at Shepherd's Yard, in Back Lane. This was the last to close, in the 1960s. It had been in the Shepherd family for 100 years, since Will Shepherd bought the business. His son Joe, a wheelwright, who followed in his footsteps, died of sunstroke in 1925 at the early age of 42, and was succeeded by his own son, also Joe. The young man worked hard to learn the wheelwright's trade and 'Eventually I gained full control in the wheelwright's shop, pleased and proud I had taken the place of my father'. In the early days of his apprenticeship he worked for three months in the paint shop with his uncle Jim, his father's partner, who was a painter and signwriter. He recalled:

> I well remember having to take off my boots...and put on a pair of slippers to paint the inside and floor of John Inns' haycarts. Should there have been any stud marks on these floors there would have been 'hell let loose'. That was pride taken in the work.

Although the blacksmith's yard has closed, the Shepherd family's long association with it will not be forgotten, as the footpath from the High Street to the site of the smithy by the horse chestnut tree in Southend Close has

108 The wedding of Joe and Annie Shepherd in 1908, taken in Shepherd's blacksmith's yard in Church Lane.

109 Joe Shepherd, wheelwright, with a painting of Shepherd's Yard by Sid Manning, shortly before the yard was demolished to make way for Southend Close in the 1960s.

been named Shepherd's Path in their memory. Previously this path was known unofficially to local people as Hodgson's Alley, after Nathan Hodgson who invented and patented a knife cleaning machine in the 1880s from adjacent premises.

Joe Shepherd was also a volunteer fireman, a job he loved. He was delighted when the opportunity came to live in the premises attached to the fire station on the corner of Basil's Road and Church Lane. In February 1939 he and his wife moved into the accommodation which consisted of a bedroom and sitting room above the station and a small kitchen below. But their tenancy was short-lived. At the outbreak of the Second World War, the fire brigade took over the whole building and the Shepherds moved to Lawrance Avenue.

The Second World War brought troops back to the town, the Old Castle canteen re-opened, black-out regulations were strictly

enforced and five dismal years of queuing, shortages, ration books and air-raid warnings overtook the town. Its proximity to London meant that local people were able to watch with horror the sky aflame with red light as London burned in 1940. The Great Northern Railway was a target for German bombers, who fortunately did not manage to hit the Stevenage stretch, though getting perilously close at Broomin Green. Some Stevenage firemen, including Fred Halling, were called upon to help fight fires in London and other places in the South East. Men who were too old or too young to be conscripted into the armed forces, or who were in reserved occupations vital to the war effort, were called up to serve in the Home Guard or the Air Raid Precautions service. Some, like John Ashby, had a gruelling daily train journey to London, returning in crowded blacked-out trains, often hearing enemy planes overhead searching for the railway line. After a long

110 Stevenage fire brigade in 1890, standing outside the engine house next to the almshouses in Church Lane.

111 Stevenage fire brigade outside Ivy House, High Street, on the occasion of the Diamond Jubilee of Queen Victoria in 1897.

112 Volunteer fire guards in the Second World War, photographed on the Bury Mead. Standing, *left to right*: Mark Allen, Charlie Brooks, Ted Grey, Mr. Oxley, George Woods and Tom Phipps. Sitting, *left to right*: George Lines, Dick Tanner and Eddie Boorman.

and arduous day's work, including Saturdays and sometimes Sundays, they then spent evenings and often whole nights in Home Guard training.

The government's policy of evacuating children from big cities produced many evacuees to live with Stevenage families during the war. Coincidentally, the Grange became home to children from the Briar Patch Children's Home at Letchworth, whose premises had burned down. They attended St Nicholas' School nearby and together with other evacuees they swelled the numbers to

an almost unmanageable degree. But sharing accommodation, making do, re-using string, envelopes and other scarce items became second nature to everyone. There were lighter moments, including the entertainments put on by the ESA Concert Party, formed in 1942. This later developed into the Lytton Players, ably and cheerfully led by Dr. Denys Swayne. His wife, Dr. Margaret, herself gave unstinting service to the people of Stevenage and district and was never known to refuse a cry for help. At last the war ended amid general relief and the hope of a better future.

Chapter 9

Local Notables

'The heart of a town lies in its people' is an apt motto for Stevenage, implying as it does that it is the residents who give the place its life and character. Inevitably, some will become outstanding, recognised as leaders in their professions, or acclaimed in their contribution to the arts or their service to humanity. Over the centuries Stevenage has produced its fair share of eminent people whose names have become known far beyond the town.

One who literally travelled far from his birthplace was the pioneer surveyor of the Bermuda Islands, Richard Norwood. The Norwood family lived at the manor house of Cannix, which is thought to be the site of the house now known as Broomin Green Farm. Richard, son of Edward Norwood, was baptised on 15 November 1590 in St Nicholas' Church and he and his sister Elizabeth attended school in Stevenage, probably the Pettits' School on the Bury Mead. When he was ten, Richard Norwood left Stevenage and moved with his family to Berkhamsted. Because of financial problems his education was unfinished, and he left school early and went to sea. During the long voyages he managed to borrow books and teach himself mathematics and other skills, which eventually enabled him to survey the uncharted Bermuda islands. His first survey was completed between 1616 and 1617, after which he came back to England, married and lived in London for 20 years as a teacher of mathematics.

Norwood also wrote several books on navigation including *The Seaman's Practice*, published in 1637, which became a standard work. In 1638, he returned to settle in Bermuda with his wife and four children. He started a school in premises he built himself and continued to write, to practise mathematics and to make surveys. He died aged 85 in 1675, leaving behind him a journal in which he had written: 'I was born in October in the year of Our Lord 1590, at Stevenage in Hertfordshire which I reckon among the many favours of God towards me ...'.

Much of the land in Stevenage, including eventually that surrounding Richard Norwood's birthplace, was owned by the Lyttons of Knebworth House. In the 19th century a member of the Lytton family was to become well-known as a writer and a reformer, and to make an unusual contribution to the history of Stevenage. This was Edward Lytton Bulwer, born in 1803, later known as Bulwer Lytton and created the first Baron Lytton. He was a man of many interests. After the first reform bill was passed in 1833 he was elected Member of Parliament for Lincoln and later represented Hertfordshire. By that time he was established as a promising young writer of novels, plays, poetry and essays. The most widely read of his novels today are *The Last Days of Pompeii* and *The Last of the Barons*, but in his life-time he was a best-selling author. His wide circle of friends included writers, artists and actors, many of whom he invited to Knebworth House. They often came by coach, sometimes using the 'York Express' from the *Saracen's Head* in London, alighting at the *Roebuck*, Broadwater, where they were met by a phaeton from Knebworth House.

One of Lytton's closest friends was Charles Dickens; Lytton had been among the first to

113 The Guild of Literature and Art building in London Road, shortly before its demolition in 1960.

114 The old schoolroom at Alleyne's School, photographed in 1905, showing plaster reliefs by Harry Bates.

recognise Dickens' genius. The two had many interests in common, notably a love of amateur theatricals and a strong desire for social reform. They both had particularly deep sympathy for struggling young writers and artists. In 1850, during a festival of amateur dramatics at Knebworth, they planned the Guild of Literature and Art, a charity to provide grants and rent-free accommodation for writers and artists. Lytton donated a plot of land by the Six Hills on the outskirts of Stevenage. He wrote a play, entitled *Not so bad as we seem*, which Dickens took on a fund-raising tour together with a farce of his own. The tour was a great success, raising £4,000 and apparently inspiring much support for the project.

On 15 June 1861 Dickens returned to Knebworth and inspected the Guild Houses then being built at Six Hills. It was on this visit that he went to see James Lucas, the Hertfordshire hermit, who lived barricaded inside his house at Redcoats Green and who was the inspiration for *Tom Tiddler's Ground*, Dickens' Christmas story for 1861.

At last, on 29 July 1865, the Guild houses were formally dedicated. Dickens arrived at Stevenage station accompanied by his family and the writer Wilkie Collins. A crowd was waiting to see them, as they drove off to luncheon in the hall of Knebworth House, where 150 people were assembled. The event was reported in *The Times*, with the speeches of Dickens and Lytton printed in full. It was all too much for some of the guests who 'gradually drifted away to the tavern across the road from the Guild houses'. They went to the *Mutual Friend* public house, named to mark the friendship between Lytton and Dickens.

Sadly, after all the hard work and generosity, the Guild of Literature and Art was a failure. It proved impossible to attract suitable residents and in 1897 the property was sold and the proceeds divided between the Royal Literary Fund and the Artists' General Benevolent Institution.

There are reminders in present-day Stevenage of Dickens' visits here. The original *Mutual Friend* was pulled down to make way

for the New Town Centre, but a modern public house in Broadwater Crescent has been given the same name. In the centre of Symonds Green housing area the *Tom Tiddler's Tavern* commemorates both the Hermit of Redcoats and Dickens' story about him. The spirit of the Knebworth theatricals continues in the aptly named Lytton Players amateur dramatic society.

While Stevenage basked in the reflected glory of Knebworth's literary heyday, the birth of another great man took place in a little house near Stevenage station. Ellen Terry, then unknown but later to become a famous actress, had been living near Wheathampstead with Edward Godwin. She arranged to stay in a midwife's house in Railway Street (now 23 Orchard Road) for the birth of her second child on 16 January 1872. The boy was named Edward Gordon Craig and he grew up to become one of the greatest theatrical designers of all time. His best known book, *The Art of the Theatre*, is still studied today. His connection with Stevenage is commemorated in the Gordon Craig Theatre, appropriately sited near the new railway station in the town centre.

Between 1641 and 1646 Henry Chauncy was a pupil at Alleyne's Grammar School, during The Civil War period. A lifetime of research resulted in the publication of his *Historical Antiquities of Hertfordshire* in 1700, making him the county's first historian. Although nobody could have been aware of it at the time, no less a person than King Charles I passed the outskirts of Stevenage as, disguised as a servant, he made his escape from the Roundhead troops besieging Oxford. The King used the old Roman road from St Albans through Wheathampstead, Fishers Green and Corey's Mill to Baldock, thus avoiding Stevenage High Street: but no doubt the news of a royal traveller's presence soon reached the town. Chauncy described it 50 years later.

Two hundred years after Chauncy, another gifted boy was at school at Alleyne's. This was Harry Bates, born in 1850, whose family lived almost next door to the school. His father Joseph was a prosperous builder and his elder sons followed him into the family firm. Harry was expected to do the same and was apprenticed locally as a stone carver for two years before going to the Lambeth School of Art in London. He soon discovered a talent for sculpture, specialising in relief work. In 1883 he won a Royal Academy Gold Medal and travelling scholarship for a relief panel entitled *Socrates teaching the people in the agora*. The scholarship enabled him to study in Paris under the great sculptor August Rodin.

Bates became established as the leading English relief sculptor. As well as being exhibited regularly at the Royal Academy, his work was also photographed to illustrate Latin and Greek textbooks. He received commissions from wealthy patrons of the arts, including the Earl of Wemyss, and for public statues. His statue of Pandora holding her casket is on permanent display in the Tate Gallery.

In 1892, Harry Bates was elected an Associate of the Royal Academy. His old school is proud to have on display the plaster casts of three of his reliefs, the only example of his work in Stevenage, apart from a small sketch in Stevenage Museum.

The property now known as Rooks Nest House lies on the northern outskirts of Stevenage and had for at least 300 years been owned and farmed by the Howard family, being referred to in all local records and maps as 'Howards' or 'Mr. Howard's'. In 1882, probably driven out by the disastrous decline in farming at the time, the last Howards left, selling their property to Colonel Wilkinson of Chesfield Park, whose land was adjacent. At the same time the name of the property was changed to Rooks Nest House. Next door the larger and more prosperous Rooks Nest Farm, owned by the Franklin family, survived the difficult years.

It was to Rooks Nest House, the former 'Howards', that the young widow Lily Forster brought her four-year-old son, Edward Morgan Forster, in 1883. They stayed for 10 years and Forster loved the place, in spite of its loneliness, non-existent water supply, and other discomforts. He later wrote that, as soon as he arrived at Rooks Nest, 'I took it to my heart and wished I could live there for ever'.

Although he was very happy at Rooks Nest, Forster's boyhood was marred by miserable times at boarding school, culminating in a disastrous two weeks at the Grange School in Stevenage High Street. These experiences were later recalled in his semi-autobiographical novel *The Longest Journey*.

E.M. Forster became one of the greatest novelists of the 20th century, whose work, dealing as it does with social and moral dilemmas still current today, is read and studied throughout the world. In recent years his novels have been introduced to an even wider public in film versions: *A Passage to India*, directed by David Lean, and *A Room with a View*, *Howard's End*, *Maurice* and *Where Angels Fear to Tread*, all made by Merchant Ivory.

Howard's End, the novel which established Forster's reputation in 1910, is largely set in Stevenage (called Hilton in the book) and centres around the old house Howards End, which symbolises England. Apart from its literary qualities, *Howard's End* is Forster's tribute to his childhood home and the surrounding countryside which meant so much to him.

After the Second World War Forster lent his support to those who were trying to protect the countryside between Chesfield, Graveley, St Nicholas' Church and Rooks Nest from development. Eminent scholars and others from four continents joined the campaign and, in 1974, the *Guardian* newspaper coined the name 'Forster Country', which now has official recognition as the name of this 'little piece of England' to the north of Stevenage.

While the Forsters were living in Stevenage, Rector Jowitt and his wife Louisa rejoiced at the birth of their son William in 1885. Following a successful academic career at Oxford, he became a brilliant lawyer, of whom it was said, 'In the courts he argued the matters in which he appeared with precision and force and his clear presentation of a case gave it a perspective which was of

115 E.M. Forster, seen here aged four, on his arrival at Rooks Nest in 1883.

116 Rooks Nest House, 1980. Inscribed on the slate wall plaque are the words: 'E.M. Forster, Elizabeth Poston, Clementine Poston ... lived here and loved this place'.

117   Elizabeth Poston seen here in the 1930s.

of a New Town at Stevenage. He died in 1957, and as he had no sons the title died with him. For many years his only memorials in Stevenage were the Sish Lane flats named Jowitt House and Chancellor's Road, parallel with Rectory Lane, his former home. Eventually in 1991 a service was held in St Nicholas' Church, where his father had been rector, to dedicate a memorial plaque in his name.

On 24 October 1905 Elizabeth Poston was born at Highfield, Pin Green. Her parents, Charles and Clementine Poston, were friends of the Forsters and the unwitting prototypes for the characters of Charles and Ruth Wilcox in *Howard's End*. Charles Poston, who had contributed much to Stevenage, died in 1913. By a strange twist of fate, the following year the widowed Clementine Poston, her daughter Elizabeth and son Ralph, found themselves living at Rooks Nest House as tenants of the Poyntz-Stewarts of Chesfield.

From babyhood it was clear that Elizabeth Poston had remarkable musical gifts, which led her to a career as a composer, broadcaster and writer. She became a Fellow of the Royal Academy of Music, working closely with Vaughan Williams, Peter Warlock and other leading composers. One of her great interests was the study of folksong, about which she became an authority. Among other work, her collections of Christmas carols, published by Penguin, are now regarded as definitive.

No less important was her work at the B.B.C. During the Second World War she had a unique position in the BBC's European Service, working directly under Churchill and the War Office for the liberation of the allied countries. Her rôle, which she later described as 'secret service agent', included broadcasting coded messages via gramophone records. After the war she played an important part in the founding and development of the BBC's Third Programme.

Elizabeth Poston continued to live at Rooks Nest, which she was eventually able to buy, until the end of her life. Always eager to take up new musical challenges, she was looking forward to starting work on a

much assistance to the juries'. Jowitt was a controversial figure, known in some quarters as the 'Vicar of Bray'. Elected Liberal MP for Preston in 1929, he was then asked to accept the appointment of Attorney-General in the Labour Government. He resigned his seat, stood again as a Labour candidate and was re-elected for the same constituency. He resigned as Attorney-General in 1932, after being defeated when he stood as a National Labour Candidate for the Combined English Universities. When Labour was returned to office in 1945, William Jowitt was made Lord Chancellor and was later created Vicount Jowitt, assuming the title Lord Stevenage.

Jowitt's expert assistance was invaluable in promoting the legislation to enable the building

collection of Russian folksongs when she died aged 81 in 1987. Still much missed in Stevenage, she lives on in her music and it is with a special thrill that her friends hear, during the annual Christmas Service of Nine Lessons and Carols from King's College, Cambridge, the pure notes of her best known carol, *Jesus Christ the Apple Tree*.

In a continuation of the musical tradition, Rooks Nest House was occupied for a few years after Elizabeth Poston's death by Dr. Malcolm Williamson, Australian-born Master of the Queen's Music, who contributed to the cultural life of Stevenage and gave whole-hearted support to the continued campaign to protect the Forster Country from development.

In 1954 Tom Hampson came to Stevenage as Social Relations Officer for the Development Corporation. He was a world-class athlete, entirely self-trained. His distinguished athletics career included winning the 800 metres race in the 1930 Empire Games, the gold medal for the same distance in the 1932 Olympics at Los Angeles, in which he set a world record time of 49.7 seconds, and a silver medal in the men's 400 metres relay. In recognition of these achievements and of the help and encouragement he gave to young sportsmen, Hampson Park was named after him following his death in 1965.

Of many political figures associated with Stevenage, two may be mentioned. In 1978 Dame Evelyn Denington was raised to the

118 Shirley Williams (standing on the left) opening the Whitney Wood Fête, *c*.1970. Standing on the right is the Rev. Ernest Wimpress, long-serving minister of the Stevenage United Reformed Church.

peerage and took the title of Baroness Denington of Stevenage. She had been a member of the Stevenage Development Corporation from 1950-1980, and its chairman from 1966. During these years, she gave unstinting service to the town, becoming involved in many different facets of its life. It was largely due to her support that the Stevenage Artists' Co-operative came into existence and, in acknowledgement of this, their art gallery at Springfield House is called the Denington Gallery.

Shirley Williams, who was Stevenage's M.P. from 1964 to 1979, was another public figure who devoted much time and energy to the town. In spite of heavy parliamentary commitments—she was successively Secretary of State for Prices and Consumer Protection, Paymaster General and Secretary of State for Education and Science—she was present at a wide variety of local events from the Whitney Wood Fête to the opening of the new railway station, as well as giving help and advice to individuals. In recognition of her work for Stevenage, Shirley Williams was made a freeman of the Borough in 1980.

Notable explorers, writers, musicians, politicians and many others have had associations with Stevenage. Yet it is not widely remembered now that the town was once the birthplace of a king. In the year 1690, near the Six Hills, Henry Boswell, king of the gipsies, was born. He died at the age of 90 and was buried at Ickleford. A memorial stone in the nave of St Katherine's Church records his name, but his body lies in an unmarked grave in the churchyard where, local tradition has it, primroses spring up every year.

Chapter 10

Rus in urbe

The hardship and suffering endured through the years of the Second World War did not come to an end for everyone when peace was declared. In cities, especially, thousands of homes had been bombed and there was an urgent need for the government to plan on a large scale to solve the problem. Even before the 1939-45 war it had been recognised that many of the nation's houses were in a very poor condition and something would have to be done to improve the situation.

In small country towns such as Stevenage the problem was a different one; that of providing employment opportunities to allow the community to prosper. The relationship between the needs of city and country had long been recognised by people such as Ebenezer Howard and others involved in the Garden City movement, which aimed to bring town and country together to provide the best of both. The first Garden City, at Letchworth, was an inspiration to many.

Philip Ireton, born in Walkern Road, Stevenage in 1904 and educated at Letchmore Road School, was a close observer of Letchworth's progress. He became convinced that a similar plan would be beneficial to Stevenage, even before the German bombs of the Second World War brought the plight of homeless Londoners to the nation's attention. By then he was a member of the Town and Country Planning Association and was aware of plans being drawn up to build a ring of 'satellite' towns within a 30-mile radius of London, to provide homes in a setting which would combine town and country. It was the idealist's vision, which had existed for many centuries, of *rus in urbe*—the country in the town.

The intention was to build each satellite town around an existing small town situated on major road and rail routes into London. Knebworth was one of the early choices, but it was Philip Ireton who pointed out the importance of the Hertford loop line from Stevenage to Moorgate, bypassing Knebworth, which would give Stevenage an alternative route if the Great Northern Railway were to be disrupted for any reason. The logic of this was accepted and in November 1946 Stevenage was designated Britain's first New Town.

119 Philip Ireton, CBE.

120 The town centre pond developed out of the spring and marsh at Bedwell Plash, photographed 9 August 1964.

In all the struggles, frustrations and successes of the next 50 years, Philip Ireton was closely involved. Having joined the Labour Party at the age of 14, he was elected to the Stevenage Urban District Council in 1937 and served continuously for 33 years. He was the only member of the Development Corporation to serve for the whole of its life. He was on the governing body of numerous schools and colleges, a magistrate and a member of many other local government and public committees. He became the first Labour chairman of the Hertfordshire County Council in 1973. Throughout his public career he was admired and respected by people of all political persuasions, even those most opposed to his views. The decision to confer upon him the first honorary freedom of the new Borough of Stevenage in 1975 was universally acclaimed.

No doubt Philip Ireton will be remembered by future generations in connection with the development of Stevenage as a New Town, much as Rector Thomas Alleyne is remembered for founding Alleyne's School. But, just as Thomas Alleyne was a friend and support to those who needed help in his day, so must it be recorded that Philip Ireton was not just

a committee man, a public figure; he readily helped all who turned to him and, as far as was in his power, was a friend to those in need. And he remained all his life a devoted and expert gardener, truly embodying in his own life the ideal of *rus in urbe*.

Stevenage New Town had been planned for 60,000 people. Its population is now nearly 80,000 and still growing. Had the original plan been adhered to, a satisfactory blend of town and country might well have been attained and the very great achievements of Britain's first New Town been acclaimed without reservation.

As it is, unforeseen developments, such as the building of the Chells Manor and Poplars areas, with Wellfield Wood still to come, have distorted the original plan so that Stevenage is in danger of becoming a shapeless urban sprawl across the countryside.

To redress the balance somewhat, mention must be made of the present Borough Council's commitment to conserving the open spaces within the town's boundaries and the excellent 'green' policies promoted in its 1990 District Plan. It is to be hoped that no extraneous pressures prevent them from being carried out.

121 This 1971 photograph, *above left*, shows work beginning on the Fairlands Valley Park. Cllr. James Boyd can be seen driving the earth-mover.

122 The Avenue, Stevenage, *c.*1985, *above right*, before the great storm felled many of its oldest trees a few years later.

123 Farmland in Forster Country, *below*, near St Nicholas' Church, *c.*1980.

124 Friends of the Forster Country Edwardian Walk. John Austin is addressing the crowd from the archway of the Grange in 1989.

The rôle of the Stevenage Conservation Liaison Committee, set up by the Borough Council as a channel of communication between council officials and voluntary conservation groups, is an invaluable means of fostering the concept of *rus in urbe*. When all is said and done, it is the people, acting of their own volition, who can and must protect the town's countryside. The remarkable battles fought and won in the 1970s to save Fairlands Valley are evidence of this. So, too, is the most recent victory, that of the Friends of the Forster Country in 1994. Working closely with the Borough Council through the Stevenage Conservation Liaison Committee, this group eventually succeeded in getting government agreement to modify the Green Belt boundary in order to 'protect for all time the open green space to the north of Stevenage known as the Forster Country'. There is now a more enlightened attitude towards such matters as the maintenance of public open spaces. No longer in total thrall to the concept of closely clipped grass and the eradication of 'weeds', Stevenage is beginning at last to accept the *rus* in its midst. Some grass verges are now free to blossom with dandelions, daisies and speedwell, just as the old meadows did for centuries. Most delightfully, the Avenue's thistles and hedgerow plants are being allowed to flourish and run to seed, so that nowadays one is almost guaranteed to see goldfinches and long-tailed tits when walking there.

Whether or not, in the words of the pioneer planners, 'something of the character of the local countryside will pervade the whole of the town itself', remains in question. But there is every reason for hope.

Appendix

Remember the men of Stevenage killed in two World Wars.

1914-1918

Lieutenant, George Abbott, Hertfordshire Regiment.

Private, Cuthbert V.W. Albone, Hertfordshire Regiment.

Sergeant, Gilbert W. Albone, Bedfordshire Regiment.

Ordinary Seaman, Frederick J. Aldridge, Royal Navy.

Private, Joseph Allen, Oxford & Bucks. Light Infantry.

Private, Leonard G. Allen, Welch Regiment.

Private, Thomas Allen, Royal Berks. Regiment.

Acting Sergeant, Frederick Ansell, Herts. Regiment.

Sergeant, Charles Anthony, King's Royal Rifle Corps.

Corporal, Frank Anthony, Rifle Brigade.

Private, William J. Arbon, East Yorks. Regiment.

2nd Air Mechanic, Frederick E. Ashwood, R.A.F.

Sapper, David Austin, Royal Engineers.

Private, Thomas S. Austin, Royal Fusiliers.

Private, George W. Barker, Leicestershire Regiment.

Private, William H. Barker, Northumberland Fusiliers.

Private, Frederick Bentley, Hertfordshire Regiment.

Private, Reuben Bradford, Bedfordshire Regiment.

Lance-Corp., Henry G. Brown, Bedfordshire Regiment.

Private, Arthur W. Bryant, Hertfordshire Regiment.

Private, William Bryant, North Staffs. Regiment.

Corporal, A. Bygrave, Bedfordshire Regiment.

Gunner, Reuben Bygrave, Royal Field Artillery.

2nd Lieut., George S. Carter, MC, East Surrey Regiment.

Lance-Corp., Albert L. Catlin, Bedfordshire Regiment.

Private, W. Noah Chalkley, Yorks. Regiment.

Sapper, Arthur Chamberlain, Royal Engineers.

Private, William Chamberlain, Border Regiment.

Shoeing Smith, Ernest Chambers, Royal Field Artillery.

Private, Seymour A. Chambers, Northumberland Regiment.

Private, William C. Clark, Lincs. Regiment.

Private, John W. Collins, East Surrey Regiment.

Rifleman, Cecil H. Cooper, Rifle Brigade.

Master-at-Arms, Edward J. Croft, Royal Navy.

Private, Charles Day, Lancs. Fusiliers.

Private, Herbert T. Day, Bedfordshire Regiment.

Sergeant Major, Alfred W. Draper, Bedfordshire Regiment.

Private, George Draper, Bedfordshire Regiment.

Corporal, Harold F. Dyke, First Surrey Rifles.

Lieutenant, George H. Eaton, 19th Hussars.

Sergeant, Alfred J. Emery, Middlesex Regiment.

Private, Frederick W. Emery, Bedfordshire Regiment.

Private, William H. Eyden, Grenadier Guards.

Rifleman, Arthur F. Fairey, Rifle Brigade.

Midshipman, Ivon G. Fellowes, Royal Navy.

Captain, Rupert C.B. Fellowes, Coldstream Guards.

Private, Alfred Forder, Bedfordshire Regiment.

Sergeant, Henry C. Forder, DCM, Bedfordshire Regiment.

Flight Lieut., Cuthbert Foster, R.A.F.

Private, John Furr, Manchester Regiment.

Private, Frederick W. Game, Bedfordshire Regiment.

Private, Cecil G. Gardner, Royal Fusiliers.

Sergeant, Harry G. Garrod, Hertfordshire Regiment.

Driver, Walter Gates, Royal Field Artillery.

Sergeant, George Gray, Hertfordshire Regiment.

Gunner, William R. Green, Royal Garrison Artillery.

Captain, Harry H. Grigg, Gurkha Rifles.

Private, G. Haggar, Bedfordshire Regiment.

Private, Cecil G. Hawkes, Essex Regiment.

Private, Robert Hemmings, Machine Gun Corps.

Private, Henry J. Heskins, West Riding Regiment.

Private, Harold Hewes, Middlesex Regiment.

Rifleman, Harold D. Holdron, London Rifle Brigade.

Major, H.B. Holmes, 2nd Royal Irish Fusiliers.

Private, Ernest Hornsby, Royal Marine Light Infantry.

Private, John Kirby, East Kent Regiment.

Private, W. Oscar Littlewood, Royal Fusiliers.

Private, William H.A. Lloyd, Bedfordshire Regiment.

Captain, Sidney H. Lowry, MC, Hertfordshire Regiment.

Trooper, Sidney G.Madgin, 9th Lancers.

Private, Francis A. Males, Manchester Regiment.

Private, Frank C. Manning, Royal Army Service Corps.

Private, Frederick Mardling, Canadian Infantry.

Corporal, Alfred C. Marshall, Royal Highlanders.

Private, George H.Marshall, Canadian Machine Gun Corps.

Private, John Marshall, Bedfordshire Regiment.

Private, Albert Mayne, Coldstream Guards.

Acting Sergeant, James H. Moss, Hertfordshire Regiment.

Private, Reginald J. Moss, Bedfordshire Regiment.

Sergeant, Bertram R. Newberry, Hertfordshire Regiment.

Private, Maurice A. Newberry, Hertfordshire Regiment.

Rifleman, Reginald J.Newberry, King's Royal Rifle Corps.

Lance-Corporal, George Norman, Middlesex Regiment.

Private, Frederick G. Oliver, Bedfordshire Regiment.

Lieut-Commander, Donald J.S. Oswald, Royal Navy.

Private, Herbert Palmer, Bedfordshire Regiment.

Private, David Payne, Gloucestershire Regiment.

Driver, William A. Pearce, Royal Field Artillery.

Private, Alfred Pettengell, Bedfordshire Regiment.

Private, Ernest Phipps, Bedfordshire Regiment.

Private, Leonard Piggott, Northumberland Regiment.

Private, John Pilkington, Royal Army Medical Corps.

Private, Ernest D. Poulter, Bedfordshire Regiment.

Private, John Robertson, Royal Berkshire Regiment.

Private, William A. Sams, Essex Regiment.

Sergeant, Charles E. Sangster, Bedfordshire Regiment.

Private, William C. Sapsed, Hertfordshire Regiment.

Private, Frank Saunders, Middlesex Regiment.

Lance-Corp., Frederick C. Scarborough, Duke of Cornwall's Light Infantry.

Private, Charles Sell, Border Regiment.

Gunner, Harry W. Sharman, Machine Gun Corps.

Gunner, Frank A. Shelford, Royal Field Artillery.

Lance-Corp., Frederick Shelford, Bedfordshire Regiment.

Corporal, Harry J. Shelford, Tank Corps.

Sapper, James Smith, Bedfordshire Regiment.

Lance-Corp., William A. Smith, Bedfordshire Regiment.

Acting Sergeant, Percy H. Snellgrove, MM, Herts. Regiment

Private, Robin Snoxell, Royal Fusiliers.

Private, Walter Street, Border Regiment.

Private, Ernest Taplin, Bedfordshire Regiment.

Private, Nelson Taplin, Royal West Kent Regiment.

Private, Harold R. Tavener, Canadian Infantry.

Writer, Ernest R. Titmuss, Royal Navy.

Private, Ernest W. Tooley, Leicestershire Regiment.

Lance-Corp., Frederick Waldock, Royal Sussex Regiment.

Private, George L. Waldock, Notts. & Derby Regiment.

Lieutenant, Horatio S. Walpole, Coldstream Guards.

Private, C.W. Ward, Bedfordshire Regiment.

Sergeant, Walter Warren, Artists' Rifles.

Private, Alfred J. Welch, Hertfordshire Regiment.

Private, Frederick Welch, Bedfordshire Regiment.

Private, F. Cyril Westwood, Bedfordshire Regiment.

Private, Horace F.Wheatley, Royal West Surrey Regiment.

Trooper, Henry J. Wilson, Hertfordshire Yeomanry.

Private, George Wright, King's Own Scottish Borderers.

1939-1945

Private, Owen C.H. Abbiss, Dorset Regiment.

Bombardier, Jack S. Allen, Royal Artillery.

Flight Sergeant, Harold B. Batchelor, R.A.F.

Sergeant, John F. Bates, R.A.F.

Private, Philip Seager Berry, Home Guard.

Aircraftsman, Donald E. Blow, R.A.F.

Flying Officer, Michael Briden, R.A.F.

Private, S. Cross, Beds. & Herts. Regiment.

Lance Bombardier, George W. Chambers, Royal Artillery.

Lance Bombardier, Edwin R. Couldrey, Commandos.

Sergeant, Thomas Earle, R.A.F.

Sapper, William J.D. Ellis, Royal Engineers.

Private, Arthur J. Froy, Home Guard.

Acting Captain, Gordon Franklin, Royal Corps of Signals.

Lieutenant, George Gaylor, GM, Royal Engineers.

Private, Edward V. Hemmings, 6th Airborne Division.

Driver, Frederick A. Hill, Royal Army Service Corps.

Private, Oliver G. Jeffs, Suffolk Regiment.

Private, Wiliam J. Jenkins, Dorset Regiment.

Corporal, Ralph W. Lines, Sherwood Foresters.

Gunner, Jim Moules, Royal Artillery.

Lieutenant, Barry S. Newton, King's Royal Rifle Corps.

Captain, Charles W.R. Oddie, Royal Artillery.

Aircraftsman, Kenneth I. Oliver, R.A.F.

Sub-Lieutenant, Alan A. Pollock, Fleet Air Arm.

Warrant Officer, Kenneth A.G. Prater, R.A.F.

Gunner, Harry Rowbottom, Royal Artillery.

Pilot Officer, Eric L.V. Stanley, R.A.F.

Pilot Officer, Alec Stevens, R.A.F.

Lieutenant, Ian B. Tetley, Royal Navy.

Lance-Corp., Gordon G.R. Upton, Royal Engineers.

Corporal, Allan H. Ward, 15th Reconnaissance.

Private, Eric G. Ward, Queen's Royal Regiment.

Sergeant, Douglas Watson, Royal Artillery.

Flight Sergeant, Stanley Welch, R.A.F.

Gunner, William C. Welch, Royal Artillery.

Guardsman, Kenneth W. Wilderspin, Coldstream Guards.

Lieut-Colonel, Humphrey R. Woods, DSO, MC, 60th Rifles.

Flight Sergeant, Roy Worsdale, R.A.F.

Bombardier, Ronald Wright, Royal Artillery.

Bibliography

Chauncy, Sir Henry, *The Historical Antiquities of Hertfordshire* (1700)

Culley, Mabel, *A Stevenage picture book* (c.1950)

Davies, E. St Hill and Dodwell, F., *Hidden from history: women in Stevenage, 1888-1988*

De Salis, Dorothy and Stephens, Richard, 'An Innings well played', *The story of Alleyne's School, Stevenage* (1989)

Hertfordshire County Records, 'Extracts from Sessions Rolls', 1581-1698

Johnson, W. Branch, *Memorandums for ...* (1972)

Jones-Baker, Doris, editor, *Hertfordshire in History* (1991)

Lenton, Joyce, *A Stevenage Chronicle*

Methold, E.V., *Notes on Stevenage and Baldock*

Munby, Lionel, *Hertfordshire population statistics, 1663-1801* (1963)

Pitcher, June, *Sketch map of Stevenage, Herts. in 1836* (1980)

Public Record Office, *Calendar of Assize records*, Hertfordshire indictments, Elizabeth I

Public Record Office, *Calendar of Assize records*, Hertfordshire indictments, James I

Spicer, C.M., *Tyme out of mind* (1984)

Stevenage Development Corporation, *The new town of Stevenage* (1949)

Stevenage Parish Magazine, 1871-1917

Stevenage Society, *The changing face of Stevenage High Street* (1982)

Trow-Smith, Robert, *The History of Stevenage* (1958)

Urwick, William, *Non-conformity in Hertfordshire* (1884)

Viatores, *Roman roads in the south-east midlands* (1964)

Victoria County History of Hertfordshire (1902)

Young, Arthur, *General view of the agriculture of the county of Hertfordshire* (1804)

Index

Figures in **bold** refer to those pages where the illustrations occur.